Our Marriage Our Redemption

GEORGE & BERTHA TOULSON

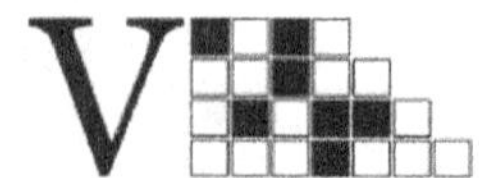

DEDICATION

I dedicate this book to our 8 children and 9 grandchildren. God has blessed us with HIS Word, which is what we leave behind. We have talents, skills and abilities that are rich but they didn't amass us money as we thought
Our examples of "A Strong Marriage" as exemplified by our lives is what we leave to you.

INTRODUCTION

This book is written to the many people who requested that we write a book, since they believed our experiences were so unique. Our Marriage was arranged -arranged by God Himself through the Holy Spirit. We were frustrated by our attempts to have the right mate in our lives. So I prayed and made a list of 53 things I wanted in a husband. This list was made with no specifications of race or looks. The most important aspect of my list was that the man had to be a born again believer and he could not be even a social drinker. – Not one teaspoon! There could not be a compromise ever again.

George and I were bankers and we individually had gone to many "cheese and wine sips" . Usually that atmosphere lends itself to "hook-ups" which take people on a slippery slope to deception. This is where I drew the line. I had married a so called "born again, holy ghost filled, drunk" according to my second husband's summation.

So for the many single women who want to have a godly marriage, our example is one of no compromise. Women over 40 believe they have to settle for whatever they can get. As a woman over 50 I found that when God's hand is on your life, He will bring your Husband to you and he will love you godly and passionately. My ideal man would not only find me but I wanted to be **petted, pampered and pursued.**   At first, I was ashamed of even thinking of another wedding but George said to me, you have to be an example to your women friends. So here I was in Philadelphia on visit with one of George's female business partners looking for a white dress, which I found in a consignment store in Chestnut Hill.

We already had adult children, but no grandchildren. After we married, two of our adult children decided they would stop their shacking up and get married instead. One had a fairytale wedding comprised of all doctors and a magistrate as attendants.

We covered the spectrum of bringing Godly principles to brides and grooms even over 50 years old. What is more remarkable is that in God, age has no real significance. My husband was 9 years younger than me.

We are parents and grandparents of many other "spiritual children". It seems God wanted us to birth Christian children. So there are many other people who call us Dad and Mom. We became the leaders of the marriage ministry at Victory Christian Fellowship. We have counseled many couples who have a multitude of issues. We found the answers in That Real Book – THE HOLY BIBLE.

- Bertha

CONTENTS

PREFACE

Our Marriage, Our Redemption

Love Said, Not So, is a BeBe Winans song that I walked up the aisle to on my wedding day in Los Angeles, California, at Crenshaw Christian Center Church, on May 6, 1995 at 1PM. I was getting married to Bertha Merlene Frazier. The song captured our life up to 1:30PM that day, for on that day and at that time, our lives forever changed. **2 Corinthians 5:17-23** sums it up. It reads:

[17] Therefore if any man be in Christ, he is a new creature: old things are passed away; behold, all things are become new. [18] And all things are of God, who hath reconciled us to himself by Jesus Christ, and hath given to us the ministry of reconciliation; [19] To wit, that God was in Christ, reconciling the world unto himself, not imputing their trespasses unto them; and hath committed unto us the word of reconciliation. [20] Now then we are ambassadors for Christ, as though God did beseech you by us: we pray you in Christ's stead, be ye reconciled to God. [21] For he hath made him to be sin for us, who knew no sin; that we might be made the righteousness of God in him.[1]

Ephesians 1:7-12 talks about **redemption.** It reads:

----

[1]*The Holy Bible : King James Version.* 1995. Logos Research Systems, Inc.: Oak Harbor, WA

7 In Him we have redemption (deliverance and salvation) through His blood, the remission (forgiveness) of our offenses (shortcomings and trespasses), in accordance with the riches *and* the generosity of His gracious favor,

8 Which He lavished upon us in every kind of wisdom and understanding (practical insight and prudence),

9 Making known to us the mystery (secret) of His will (of His plan, of His purpose). [And it is this:] In accordance with His good pleasure (His merciful intention) which He had previously purposed *and* set forth in ᶜHim,

10 [He planned] for the maturity of the times *and* the climax of the ages to unify all things *and* head them up *and* consummate them in Christ, [both] things in heaven and things on the earth.

11 In Him we also were made [God's] heritage (portion) *and* we obtained an inheritance; for we had been foreordained (chosen and appointed beforehand) in accordance with His purpose, Who works out everything in agreement with the counsel *and* design of His [own] will,

12 So that we who first hoped in Christ [who first put our confidence in Him have been destined and appointed to] live for the praise of His glory![2]

---

[2]*The amplified Bible, containing the amplified Old Testament and the amplified New Testament.* 1987. The Lockman Foundation: La Habra, CA

CHAPTER 1
IN THE BEGINNING

George, In The Beginning

In January 1994 around midnight, at age 44, I had tears running down my face. On reflection, the fact that I was unable to buy Christmas gifts for my four children (actually five children, but later for that) was the last added pressure that broke the dam holding back my tears. At that time, I felt the absolute lowest I've ever felt in my life. Was there nothing more to my life? I had determined that my life was made up of 4 segments:

1) my profession (banking)
2) my financial condition
3) my personal life
4) my children

The first three segments were in the toilet and the last one, I couldn't even buy Christmas gifts for the children. I was extremely low. Then, I heard an audible voice coming from inside of me. The voice said **"you need to be someplace else".** That's all I heard. I had never experienced anything like that in my life. Little did I know 3 months later, I'd again hear that audible voice.

At the time, I was engaged to, and living with, a very nice lady whose first name began with H. H loved me and respected me even after all I had put her through. I was an alcoholic and unfaithful. This combination was the main source of my two previous failed marriages and all told, accounted for about 25 years of my life, starting around 1970. During those 25 years there should have been countless DUI's, but officially only one. There were two totaled vehicles and numerous side-swiping of cars and many instances of minor damage to my vehicles.

In April of 1994, I left a Center City Philadelphia banking function (with an open bar) late in the evening, around 16th and Market St, totally drunk. I was driving west on Walnut Street, a large four-lane one-direction city street, where at 63rd and Walnut, I had to make a right or a left turn because there was a city park at the end of 63rd and Walnut. I didn't make either turn. What I did do was bottom out my car, due to a dip in the road surface entering into the park, and tore a hole in the oil pan as I drove between two two-foot square, approximately 7 feet high brick pillars to the entrance of the park. There was no other damage to the car, just a tear in the oil pan. After coming to a stop, I heard an audible voice say **"this is the last time".** I don't remember that exact time-frame, so I'll say some time later, I was **compelled** to go back to where this accident had occurred. I was driving a similar sized car that I drove through the two brick pillars and tore a hole in the oil pan. I could see that there wasn't a lot of room between the pillars, so I positioned the car I was driving between the two pillars, attempting to be dead-center between the brick pillars. I got out of the car and there was exactly 36 inches or 3 feet on both sides of the car. Please keep in mind, I drove **47 blocks** (16th street to 63rd street) on a **four lane one-direction city street** and somehow (I know how now) drove between two two-foot square brick pillars, and the only damage was the oil pan.

The day after the accident, I told H how sorry I was. She was in tears and at that moment I knew I had to stop hurting her. A few days later I got the courage to tell her that at the end of our lease, which was August 31, 1994, I was going to go my own way and put an end to the hurt I was causing her.

In 1992, I became President of the Philadelphia Chapter of the Urban Bankers Association (UBA) and attended my first national conference in Birmingham, Alabama. I had worked my way up through the ranks in the Philadelphia chapter, helped in growing the chapter, and enjoyed organizing and managing professional banking events in the Philadelphia area. At this national conference in June, I met the finest collection of black professionals I've ever met. I particularly liked the Los Angeles Chapter of UBA. But I was an alcoholic, and at the conference, there was an open bar in the Hospitality Suite. Needless to say, I got drunk at some point during the 1992 conference. However, I made friends with folks from the LA UBA and looked forward to seeing them again in June 1993, this time in San Diego.

Wow! San Diego! I was use to seeing the brown Atlantic Ocean off of Atlantic City, but the Pacific Ocean off of San Diego was such a pretty blue and if I looked east I could see mountains. Couple that with beautiful Hispanic women and I was mesmerized. But, I was still an alcoholic, and I got drunk. At the end of the conference in 1993, I was so disappointed in myself, but I didn't know what to do. I remember saying to myself, if this is all there is, I wouldn't be going to next year's conference.

Bertha, In The Beginning

I had been living in the Inland Empire (a huge suburb of Los Angeles) since 1984, three years after my marriage to B. He left for the last time in 1987, and I was alone, and having a rough time trying to raise Felicia, my daughter, who had become sullen most of the time, and began to cut herself and exhibit suicidal tendencies. She ran away all the time and spent time with her Father and other people. I loved her and thought this was a time for us to get closer. Felicia left and got a job and barely made it out of high school. She took her GED and was finished high school before she was to graduate.

I had gone through a time of being alone, laid off from my job, disgruntled with my church, and homeless, sleeping on the floor of a recently acquired Christian friend. She had taken me in because another woman, who worked in the same insurance company as I had, evicted me from her home. Her car had been set afire and her house could have burned down. She suspected the guy I had dated had done it. I believed she was right. She had forbidden me to see him. So, at a moments notice, I had to move and my Christian friend was so gracious to allow me to move in with her. My life was so compromised at that time.

In 1992, I returned from the Inland Empire to Los Angeles to take care of my stepmother Pennie, who was suffering from Alzheimer's. She needed me and I needed her. I had always been a caregiver and I had the awesome responsibility as executor of my Dad's estate, which included the house where Pennie was living. This was the perfect arrangement for me and it placed me in position to be where God wanted me. I did not have to pay rent, and I had acquired a contract with a non-profit, which gave me a solid income with no expenses. I performed my duties at work and was a companion to Pennie. She filled my lonely hours, though her condition was challenging.

After the mistakes I made in marrying my second husband, and defying God's Word by dating two men, I was told by God through the Holy Spirit, **"the next man you sleep with had better be your husband, or you can come home to be with Me"**. I tried to dismiss this statement as being my own thought or being from Satan. However, almost simultaneously, the phone rang. On the other end of the line was a "funeral home" solicitation call for a "pre-need" burial plan! It was 10:30 at night. I asked, "what are doing calling this time of night'? The lady said, "I don't know. I just had the urge to make the call". Needless to say, I bought the plan – just in case I needed it, but I was determined I would not defy this **"do not sleep"** order from The Lord Himself, because I had always been sensitive to my relationship with God, and had never wanted to hurt him – not in all my life.

Amidst my reeling from the initial shock of my Holy Spirit spanking when the undertaker phoned me, which I realized was from God Himself, I re-focused and began to get a vision. I knew I had been chastened. The Bible says to get a vision, and then "write the vision down, make it plain so that you might run with it." I was God's woman, and I had to act like it or die prematurely. For this reason, I began to compile a list of attributes I wanted in a husband. When this list was completed, it contained **53 attributes or traits**. I knew not to ask for a particular ethnicity. But, in my mind, I wanted a "white or Hispanic man - anything other than a black man. After two marriages, I was convinced that black men had inherent familial problems, which prevented them from being good husbands.

I settled into my new lifestyle living with my stepmom, made a schedule for myself and spent quality time communing with God. My room was perfectly situated in the back of the house. There I could see the garden in the daytime and watch the planes go out to the east coast in the dark and blessed nighttime. I dreamt each night that I would someday go east and wondered where those planes were taking people. I communed with the Lord all the time, and thanked Him for my time with Him, and for giving me an opportunity to live here at my Dad's home and in a room where he spent his life for many years. He called this room "his room". I had everything I needed in my room. My Dad's antique and beautiful roll-up desk, complete with desk amenities. A beautiful white bedroom suite, including a full dresser and armoire were in my room. There was a small closet for my clothes. A separate vanity area, connected to the beautiful pink bathroom, which had a shower and tub, plus drawers and cabinets for linen and personal items. Daddy's large screen TV was in my room. The old safe where Dad used to keep his money was there. I tried to open the safe on many occasions, with no luck, just to see if there was some residue of the cash he used to keep there. I found some of his guns and a dagger in the room. I watched TBN and other TV programs and spent many hours alone, (when I was not with my stepmom) or preparing meals and keeping her company. She liked to spend evenings in her room in the front of the house. My room was completely private and the TV could not be heard in other parts of the house; nor could my praying or talking on my on private phone be heard.

On most days, I exercised by walking up the hill on Mt. Vernon Dr. in LA and/or walking the path at the top of the hill overlooking the city. I began taking my new vitamin supplements from *Shapefast*, which gave me much more energy and I started to lose weight. I participated in multi-level marketing meetings at my house, and I attended outside meetings, as well. This provided me secondary income. Returning to Crenshaw Christian Center Church, I became a part of the Spanish Ministry, since I was fluent in Spanish, and met some solid friends there. My job at Community Financial Resource Center (CFRC) was a blessing. I was an Independent Contractor for them, and I liked what I was doing. I had been sought out by some political and community directors of non-profit organizations, due to my previous success as a community banker, and I made a choice to take the CFRC assignment, which involved making "micro loans" to new and expanding businesses. The Small Business Administration would guarantee these loans. I spent my time with outreach efforts and connected with many old friends and acquaintances in the LA area. Daddy's neighbors were glad to see me on a daily basis and were the recipients of my help in going to the store, caring for them, and maintaining the property on Mt. Vernon Dr.

Having been a former banker, there came a time when one friend told me that my old banking organization, the Los Angeles Urban Bankers Association (LAUB) was attending the national conference in Orlando, Fl in June of 1994. I was busy and did not want to attend a conference, where many times people were looking to meet and have encounters and "one night stands" with each other. At the last minute, this friend insisted we could go together. I had already planned to go see Felicia, who was living on the east coast in Laurel Md. I thought maybe I could add the Orlando trip and accomplish two things on one travel itinerary. So, I went first to Washington, DC where I met Felicia. I stayed in a Holiday Inn (in Georgetown) for a week then I went on to Orlando for another 4 days. This would be the trip that changed my life forever. I thought the travel plans were a "cut and paste" job. But, in actuality, God was orchestrating it all.

Meeting Felicia was a relief for me. I had not seen her for many months. She had left Los Angeles and moved to Laurel, MD overnight, with no previous notice. She was following a man she met in LA. Felicia had continued from age 12 to be experiencing difficulties in adjusting in school and had rebellion and disciplinary problems. By age 21 while living on her own, and many times with her Father and his second wife, and after her, his long time companion R, I heard the Lord speak to me and say, **"Get the stress and Felicia out of your life, because the man I am sending to you is a *gentle man*"**.

Felicia had made herself available to pick me up from the airport in DC She showed me a nice time. We went to see the National Monument and sat on the Capital steps and saw the band WAR perform in the square. We had lunch and had some interface, but she did not take me to where she lived. I later found that all those clothes in her car were an indication that she was living from place to place. I invited her to stay in the hotel with me, but she refused. After a couple of days, she left a note underneath my hotel door saying she was not coming back, and if I needed to get back to the airport, to contact her boyfriend S because she was going on with her life. The day before, she had tried to convince me she knew her way around town by driving fast and around and around the loop, but I was getting dizzy and seeing the same scenery over and over. I asked her to stop and get directions which made her angry. I did not see Felicia anymore. I continued to shop and sightsee in Georgetown, and took a cab to the airport when it was time for me to leave for Orlando. In my mind I said, this is it for me and Felicia. I might as well live for myself and make my own friendships, enjoy the conference, and have some fun.

It was early afternoon when I arrived in Orlando. One banker met me when I was checking in and told me to change into some of my pretty clothes because there would be a bus to come take us to happy hour. I thought the jeans I had on my new body was enough. I had not been in them long enough to change. But, I did go to my room and put on something more dressy. I did not have a chance to really enjoy settling in my beautiful room. I had to go. Getting on the bus, I saw many old friends - Betty, Jack, and Linda - plus new smiling faces and guys who looked at me like I was *hot*. What a change from the previous setting in Georgetown with Felicia. I was excited! For the first time in a while, I felt I was doing something for ME. I was not going to worry about my stepmom, or Felicia. I was going to have a great time with my peers. I deserved this trip!

There was a bus to take us bankers to a "happy hour" in Orlando at a place called *Pinky Lee's*, which was owned by Shaquille O'Neal. The hors d'oeuvres were delicious and I ate as much as I wanted - being careful not to overeat here. I had gotten in line for food, while the masses were getting drinks. My strategy was to be done early and get back on the first bus leaving for the hotel, while everyone else fraternized.

Leaving the hotel, I sat on the bus with these friends I knew. There was a man with them I did not know, who talked incessantly to my friends about some lady they mutually knew. He was not from the west coast. My prejudice about east coast men being players and drunkards came from previous conferences. So, I perceived this was an east coast man talking about an encounter he had. I had noticed him earlier standing on the curb deciding which bus he would get on. My thought then, when I first saw him, "you better hurry up and get on board buddy". As this man, who later on introduced himself as George continued to talk, I could not help but interject my comments about his situation with a lady. In fact I knew the lady. It seems this lady had rejected him at a previous conference. So, I continued to ad lib in favor of the lady.

I got back to my room to be alone. Then, I decided to go back downstairs to pick up information I needed for the conference. I met up with the friend who had invited me to come. She was with someone and beckoned for me to join them. So, we sat together and talked for a while. I left and went back to my hotel room. I read my Bible and scanned a book I bought in an airport. The name of that book was **"The Complete Book of Bible Literacy"**. I took a shower, looked at TV then went to bed.

CHAPTER 2
GEORGE – OFF TO ORLANDO

In January 1994, I've already explained my state of mind, and in April, I had the car accident. Knowing my alcoholic history, I really didn't want to go to Orlando for the 1994 UBA conference. I was getting really tired of the alcoholic scene. However, a good friend of mine, who happened to be my boss, strongly suggested I go, since I was a past President of the Philadelphia chapter. So, I went. It was good the see the Los Angeles UBA group. On the first night of the conference, the group took several buses to Shaquille O'Neal's club. Once we got on the bus, two ladies from the LA UBA, Betty and Yvonne, were sitting in the seat in front of my friend Jack and me. The ladies were having a good time at my expense, remembering how in 1993 in San Diego, they tried to set me up with one of their chapter's lady friend and it was a disaster. They were howling in laughter and I vaguely remember there was a lady sitting in front Betty and Yvonne who would make some comments also. But I didn't pay this lady any attention.

The next day at the UBA luncheon, I'm looking around the room, still marveling at the fine collection of black banking professionals, when I notice this woman looking at me and she's not smiling. I look away, but in a few seconds I look back at this woman. She still is looking at me and she still is not smiling. Well, I make idle conversion with a few of the people at the table and I'm sure 30 seconds have elapsed and look over at this woman again, and she's still looking at me and still not smiling! At this point, I'm thinking I must have done or said something to her, perhaps while I was drinking. And of course, I can't wait for the luncheon to be over so I can ask her why she has been looking at me and not smiling. The luncheon is over and I get distracted talking to some people when out of the corner of my eye, I see her walking past me a little ways away.

Later that evening, many of the men and women at the conference are relaxing and having a few drinks in this beautiful indoor atrium. I have a drink in my hand and I'm making the rounds with my patented "hello, my name is George" as I introduce myself to the ladies. Well, you guessed it. I finally see the mystery woman who was looking at me during the luncheon. Of course, I say "hello my name is George", and she says I know your name. I ask her how she knows my name. She says "I was talking to you last night on the bus" (the lady sitting in front of Betty and Yvonne). To that I responded, "I don't remember talking to you". To which she responded, "Negro please"! So went my introduction to Bertha Merlene Frazier, my future wife to be in exactly 11 months to the day we met. Interestingly, her response didn't phase me. And the only thing I remember saying to her was asking her to come up to the UBA Hospitality suite later that evening.

Head-rub

The hospitality suite is where most of the conferences' adjourned late in the evening. It was the place where old acquaintances from different UBA chapters got together over drinks and hors d'oeuvres. There was also the Bid Whiz card table, where trash talking and backing it up with "Six Specials" and "Six No Trumps" stirred up the 'wolfin'. I was waiting for my turn at the Bid Whiz table, and I hadn't selected a partner yet. Guess what happened next? I was actually wandering over by the door and it opened, and there was Bertha Merlene Frazier! Like I had been knowing her all my life, I slide my left arm down her right arm until I intertwined our fingers, told her she was my Bid Whiz partner, and proceeded to walk over to the Bid Whiz table just as the losers were getting up from their chairs.

Bid Whiz is similar to Spades, except your partner is there to help you win "books" or help you "set" your opponents during a game. If you and your partner win all the "books" (or hands, there are 13) in a game, that's called a "head-rub" and you rub your opponents head! Depending on how much you bid determines how many "books" your opponent needs to "set" you to lose the game. The object of the game is to get to 7 points. If, for example, you bid a "4" and your opponent doesn't win at least 4 books, you win the game and earn 4 points toward you 7 needed to win. If you bid a "5" and your opponent doesn't win at least 3 books, you win the game. With a "6" it's at least 2 books. Well, Bertha and I won 7 straight games, one of which was a head-rub. Every card I needed, she had, and every card she needed, I had. It was beautiful! Up until she played the role of Cinderella on me. After we got up from the table and smiled and hugged each other, I decided to excused myself and get a drink and asked her what I could get her. See said "nothing". I'll be right back I said, but when I returned, Bertha was no where to be found! Oh well, I went about seeing who else I knew or wanted to meet. Later on that evening, I got drunk. This was Wednesday night. On Thursday, I stayed in my room all day, eating, drinking, and watching movies, missing all the UBA events of Thursday. Hangovers will do that to you!

Foot Massage

On Friday, I went to several of the functions, but didn't see Bertha at any of them. The main function for Friday evening was the "Back to Africa" event, where African attire was the theme of the event. All I had to wear was a very nice olive green suit. As I was approaching the ballroom, at the door, as if she were waiting for me, was a smiling Cinderella. I don't remember asking her where she went two nights ago, I was just happy to see her. Bertha was all decked-out in her African garb. I apologized for not having any African attire, so she walks over to a table where African garb was being sold and bought me a very nice African scarf, that went very well with my suit. We walked into the ballroom and sat down together. The event was very colorful and festive, but the music of Marvin Gaye and other on-time artist, had the place jumping. Bertha and I were dancing and sweating. After being on the floor for what seemed a very long time, we sat down. After a few minutes, Bertha complained that her feet hurt. Never giving it a second thought, I removed her shoes and gently massaged both feet. It never occurred to me that at a Ball was probably not the time to massage her feet. *Months later, I'd find out how significant massaging her feet was to her.* At the end of the evening, I walk her to her room and she invites me in. I didn't think anything of it. On the table I notice a book entitled **"The Complete Book of Bible Literacy"**, by Mark D. Taylor. Little did I know that this book would play a pivotal part in my life, which I'll talk about later. Bertha mentioned to me that she was planning on leaving the next day, Saturday. Of course I didn't want her to leave, so I asked her to stay until the event was over on Sunday, and go with me to the Universal Studios Theme Park Saturday morning. She said she'd let me know in the morning and I left. We agreed to meet for breakfast.

Sparks Fly

At breakfast, Bertha mentioned that a friend from the LA UBA chapter had agreed to let her spend Saturday night with her, so now we were set to go to the park. Our plan was to go to the same morning session, but not sit together. We would leave separately, so not to raise suspicion, and meet the bus just outside of the lobby that would take us to the theme park. Everything went fine and we got to the park. As we were walking to the entrance of the park, we began to hold hands. That's when the sparks started to fly! Man, what an indescribable feeling!!! I did my best to put my feeling into words to her, but I know my words were so inadequate. We rode on many rides and as soon as we got off the rides we were back to holding hands. This went on all day! We knew when the bus was going to pick us and one of the stops before getting back to the hotel was a nearby shopping mall. We got off the bus at the mall because Bertha wanted to get her son some cologne. We're walking and holding hands and as we turn the corner, there was Jack, Betty, and Yvonne. We were busted! I can still remember the look on their faces. Probably, the look on their faces was because they knew me and they knew Bertha. I'm sure in their eyes we were the complete opposite of each other and nobody would have suspected us being together. Of course the question was, "what is happening here?", to which we gave a shrug of our shoulders, because we really didn't know what was going on. It just felt so good!!! We surely would have liked to have been the proverbial "fly on the wall" to their conversation.

Since Saturday was the last full day of events, there was going to be a black-tie gala that evening. Normally, members of each chapter would sit together, but I asked Bertha to sit with me and the Philadelphia chapter, which she did. We had a wonderful time and the folks from the Philadelphia and the LA chapters were looking at us and buzzing about us. After eating and dancing, and gleefully ignoring all the questions being asked, we found a little corner of the hotel and just talked.

Good-bye Kiss

Sunday was going home day. Bertha and I had very different ideas of what the next day (Monday) would bring. In her mind, she figured she'd never see me again, but in my mind, I knew I was going to call her on Monday. I helped her gather all her luggage and went with her to the airport. I asked her for a kiss and she reluctantly (or so it seemed) gave me one kiss on the lips.

Bertha's Feelings After She Left The Conference

After I left the Urban Banker's conference, George rode on the shuttle with me to the airport. He had been so sweet to help me with the daunting task of getting my bags to the airport. He asked me for a goodbye kiss. I did not want to kiss him because the smell of alcohol and his breath repulsed me. One of my parting comments to George at the airport was: When you are ready to be married, give me a call. His response was, "how do I know if we are compatible?" I then said God knows everything about me, and you can find me in the **secret place of the Most High God!** (quoting Psalms 91, my favorite scripture). I know this was baffling to him, but away I went. I had no intentions of ever seeing him again. He said he would call me on Monday, but I did not take him seriously. I really had no expectations whatsoever. So, when the phone rang at work on Monday, MQ, who was my assistant, announced George was on the phone. I asked, "George who"? When I picked up the phone, I was shocked to say the least. I did not know his last name. We talked for a while and he reminded me that he had promised to call me. So this was the beginning of many communications we would have.

Now communications with George Ronald Toulson Sr. were added to my day. Truly I found George to be a gentle man. He never used a curse word. He was educated and had a fine job with the bank. On my list of 53 things, at the top was a non-drinker. George drank. That was a deal breaker. My second husband was a drunk and alcoholic of grand proportions. The years of hell in that marriage had come to finality. I discovered he was still married to his first wife when we married, so in fact I was a victim of bigamy. I hated alcoholics, so George, at first glance could not have been husband. We talked everyday, and I believed it was my duty as a Christian woman to send him books. I knew he was an avid reader and had a hunger for The Word. Beyond that, I had no vision of marriage to him, but that was about to change.

You see, George began to speak into my spirit as if he knew the Word of God. At least, it sounded as if he did because what he spoke was beginning to tantalize my spirit. He wrote many letters and poetry and I began to be mesmerized by the communications we were having. Phone conversations and letters took on a different tone. He sent faxes to my office and MQ, along with the people in the office, were racing to the fax machine to get a glimpse of our communications. At one point MQ asked me if I was sure that George was not the man God promised me. She said, **"check your list. I think George is your husband"**. I said no he is not because he drinks. I began to speak with the group in my

Spanish Ministry about George. At one point, one lady prophesied in Spanish saying, "**He is your Husband!** The other group members felt the same.

CHAPTER 3
GEORGE – BEING LED BY THE HOLY SPIRIT

Before I begin this part of the story, I need to make a point of reference. At this point, more specifically, Monday, June 6, 1994, I didn't know that I was being lead by the Holy Spirit. The only thing I knew was I liked Bertha. I say it like this because up until now, when I looked at women, I looked at them first as a sexual object. In other words, I lusted after them. Sex was the first thing on my mind. But this time with Bertha, sex didn't cross my mind. I just liked her. I never even thought about why I liked her. I know why I liked her now, as I write this, but I'll come back to this point later on. Back to the story.

I called Bertha from my job, (which was CoreStates Bank in Philadelphia) on Monday, just like I knew I would. She was working at Community Financial Resource Center (CFRC) in Los Angeles, CA, as an independent contractor. She was surprised to hear from me. I don't remember how long we talked or what we talked about. The next day I wrote the first of many letters, faxes, poetry, and post cards to come. These letters, faxes, and poetry are the actual documents. I scanned them for this writing.

June 7, 1994

Dear Bertha,

I can't remember the last time I wrote a letter to someone. I had a business meeting scheduled for 8pm Monday night, so I stayed at the office to write to you. You really seemed surprised and glad to hear from me yesterday. That made me feel good.

I can't adequately tell you how much I really enjoyed being with you at the conference. INSEPARABLE. I wonder if God has that in store for us. Only time will tell.

I know already that you are SPECIAL. I think I knew that the moment you held my hand in the hospitality suite. Maybe that's because I'm so sensitive (smile). Also, your smile "1ights up" your whole face, and I can't help but smile too.

It's exciting to think of seeing you again. I called Northwest Airlines, just to get a feel for the airfare price, and they told me it was $401 as of today, if I travel Monday - Thursday. If I travel 20,000 miles (3.3 times to LA), I'll get a free trip. So, think about where we can travel when I attain those 20,000 miles.

Following are "vitals" you'll need to communicate with me:

Address: CoreStates

First Pennsylvania Bank

1500 Market Street

PO Box 7618

F. C. 1-3-16-20 Philadelphia, PA 19101-7618

Well, that will do it for the first letter. If you can think of any other "high tech" way of communicating, let me know.

Love,
  George

I faxed this letter to her on June 7, 1994.

Notable lines from this letter:

1)   "INSEPARABLE. I wonder if God has that in store for us. Only time will tell".
2)   "So, think about where we can travel when I attain those 20,000 miles".

Also notice that God is mentioned in my very first letter to Bertha!

****

On Wednesday, June 8th, I wrote the following letter:

June 8, 1994

Dear Bertha

I was thinking about you as I learn WordPerfect for Windows. I said to myself, why not write her as I learn. So, I'm killing two "birds" with one stone (you're the finest "bird" I know). I hope you had a good day yesterday. I also wonder what your thoughts were when you received the fax Tuesday morning.

All day long yesterday, I thought about how much I wanted to talk to you. I'm not suggesting you get another phone line for your fax, but if you did, you could expect a few faxes a day from me. A better idea though would be for both of us to get on

CompuServe. This way, we could communicate using our PC's. You would need a modem of course. I'll look into CompuServe today.

Tuesday, I interviewed a CoreStates co-worker of mine who is Chinese/Vietnamese to find out if she and her husband would be interested in meeting with me to discuss the business. I informed her that the Asian market is growing dramatically. I told her the business I'm involved with already has markets in Japan, Hong Kong, Taiwan, Korea, and Malaysia. I informed her that the business I'm associated with will be opening in China in 1995 and that I was looking to make some contacts with people of Asian nationality. She is open-minded and curious about what business I'm talking about. I hope her husband is also. Her husband is a mechanical engineer working for the Navy. The Naval shipyard is scheduled to close in 1996 and he's concerned about a job. My plan is to get them started in business in the U.S. and help them reach the Direct Distributor level. During this time, I will suggest to them that they make contacts and build relationships with people in China and other Asian countries. This way, when China opens, we'll be in a position to expand our business there.

Enough of business. I miss your smile. I particularly enjoy holding hands with you. I also remember how you would put your hand on my shoulder. It felt wonderful to be touched so affectionately. I'm someone who enjoys giving, as I believe you are also. It will be one of God's blessings if we are allowed to experience more of what we experienced in Orlando. But, even if that's not to be, I thank Him for bringing you into my life.

You excite me Bertha! A possible future with you excites me more. Only time will tell.

I hope this letter brings joy into your heart. It brought joy to my heart just writing it.

Love, George

I faxed this letter to her on Wednesday, June 8th.

Notable lines from this letter:

1)   "It will be one of God's blessings if we are allowed to experience more of what we experienced in Orlando. But, even if that's not to be, I thank Him for bringing you into my life".

2)   "You excite me Bertha! A possible future with you excites me more. Only time will tell".

3)   "I hope this letter brings joy into your heart. It brought joy to my heart just writing it."

God is mentioned a second time in as many letters!

****

I wrote the next letter on Thursday June 9th:

June 9, 1994,

Dear Bertha,

Good morning, my California Sunshine! Here are five ways we can communicate, listed by cost effectiveness and usefulness. I'll be sending you information today regarding the voice messaging service I use in the business (AMVOX) and CompuServe. I have to get the voice messaging order form, and I'll send it ASAP.

The five ways of communicating are:

*Amvox Network Voice Messaging

*24 hour messaging
* Message/Reply is up to 2 minutes
* 2 minutes will cost $.30
* Retrieval of messages from anywhere in the u.S.
* 5 day message retention

*CompuServ Information Services

* $8.95 flat monthly rate for "Basic Services"
* "Extended Services" have an hourly connect cost, and some have premium surcharges

*Fax (daily, weekly)

* Phone (I'll limit my calls to you to twice a week, if possible, 15 minute maximum)

*U.S. Mail

My rationale for listing AMVOX, followed by CompuServe is the following:
* AMVOX will allow us to hear each other in our own voice, 24 hours a day with the ability to reply quickly
* CompuServe (electronic mail) can be used to document thoughts, questions, concerns, and issues
I feel proud of being creative in thinking of ways to communicate with you. You, make me feel proud! Proud because someone as beautiful inside, as well as outside like you, cares so much for me. That feeling makes a man put "pep in his step, and glide in his stride!"

Love,
  George

I faxed this letter on June 9th.

Notable lines from this letter:

"I feel proud of being creative in thinking of ways to communicate with you. You, make me feel proud! Proud because someone as beautiful inside, as well as outside like you, cares so much for me. That feeling makes a man put "pep in his step, and glide in his stride!"

****

On June 9th, I received this fax from Bertha:

June 9, 1994

GT:

I just wrote the whole thing and lost it, so I am doing it again before 2:30.

It occurred to me how important your faxes are to me and how much I enjoy reading them over and over again; So, I decided I would also send faxes to you. So bear with me as I try to reciprocate your love and affection via fax.

Hopefully, you did receive my letter and brochures and the note I sent to you by U.S. Mail.

It seems much time has passed since our meeting. It seems we have known each other for months. I miss touching you and I miss your taking over and doing things for me that I normally would have to do for myself - Like handling my bags. It feels good just to be a woman because I have a real man.

I should get the film developed this week, and will send copies to you. This will enhance the memories we have of each other.

I am praying for you and I will look for a Bible teaching church where you will grow in faith and learn to communicate with God specifically about those things which concern us. Keep your faith on "M" for Miracle.

Te amo mi corazon

Bertha

Notable lines from this letter:

1)   "It seems much time has passed since our meeting. It seems we have known each other for months. I miss touching you and I miss your taking over and doing things for me that I normally would have to do for myself – Like handling my bags. It feels good just to be a woman because I have a real man".

2)   "I am praying for you and I will look for a Bible teaching church where you will grow in faith and learn to communicate with God specifically about those things which concern us. Keep your faith on "M" for Miracle".

In Bertha's first letter to me, there is God again, showing up in a letter. It seems Bertha and I are giving God the credit.

****

I wrote and faxed the next letter on Monday, June 13th:

Monday, June 13, 1994

Dear Bertha,

You brought up an intriguing subject when you mentioned your believe in the order of God, the man, and the wife in a marriage. I can't think of a greater responsibility that I could have for anyone. I was ignorant of that responsibility when I was married before. Now I know. I believe that God has be working on me for a while now, getting me to the point of knowing and accepting the responsibility of marriage. I accept the responsibility.

You are far ahead of me spiritually. I don't expect to reach your level, but I'll be rooted in the word.

I know we're getting ahead of ourselves regarding husband and wife, but I wanted it said that I understand and gladly accept the responsibility if you said "yes." This is not a proposal (smile). You'll know if and when I propose to you.

Love,

George

Notable lines from this letter:

This whole letter is notable! But I believe even more notable is what you may not have noticed. It took just 6 days for "marriage" to appear in our letters. And, I essentially asked her to marry me!

****

I wrote and faxed the next letter on Tuesday, June 14th:

June 14, 1994

Dear Bertha,

I believe I understand how you feel about me, my situation, and you. Perhaps if I were you, I'd feel the same way too. You are blessed that you are "free & clear" of financial, personal, and other problems of life. I'm struggling to be "free & clear" also, and I will be! I'm not asking you to burden yourself or get caught up in any of my situations. I am asking you to look beyond today and see us as we can be tomorrow. I love you and I'm asking you, to use your words, wait for me. I wasn't looking for you, but I was looking for someone for close to a year now. I've found that someone. That someone is you. You love me too, or else you wouldn't have reacted the way you did Saturday and Sunday. Dare to believe in us, even now. I promise I won't let you down.

Love,

George

Notable lines from this letter:

1)   The first mention in any letters to date – I love you…

2)   "I believe I understand how you feel about me, my situation, and you. Perhaps if I were you, I'd feel the same way too".

Bertha and I had talked earlier in the evening and I mentioned the fact that I was still living with H. This did not go over well with Bertha Merlene! This was the reason for the tone and demeanor of this letter.

****

I wrote and faxed this letter on June 15th:

June 15, 1994

My California Sunshine,

Although you are over 3000 miles away, I on the east coast and you and the west coast, I feel it's just a matter of time until we are together as one.

I think of you often during the course of a day, and I find myself always looking for something that I can relate to you. Last night, I was looking through the index of a book called, AND I QUOTE. I saw a chapter on LOVE, and I thought of you. I scanned the index further and I saw a chapter on MARRIAGE, and I thought of you. I thought I would share some of the quotes on marriage with you. I hope you enjoy them as much as I did.

"There is no more lovely, friendly, and charming relationship, communion, or company than a good marriage."

"There is no greater excitement than to support an intellectual wife and have her support you. Marriage is a partnership in which each inspires the other, and brings fruition to both of you."

"To keep the fire burning brightly, there's one easy rule: keep the two logs together, near enough to keep each other warm and far enough apart--about a finger's breadth--for breathing room. Good fire, good marriage, same rule."

" ... to have and to hold from this day forward, for better, for worse, for richer, for poorer, in sickness and in health, to love and to cherish, till death do us part."

I love you, my California sunshine.

Love,

George

Notable lines from this letter:

I was looking through the index of a book called, AND I QUOTE. I saw a chapter on LOVE, and I thought of you. I scanned the index further and I saw a chapter on MARRIAGE, and I thought of you.

****

I wrote and faxed this letter on Friday, June 17th.

June 17, 1994

Dear Bertha,

This morning, I asked H if she had been praying, because she is going through some difficult times. Her response was, "praying for what"? I felt sorry for her, because she doesn't know the power of prayer. It also reaffirms my knowledge that God does answer prayer, because he is answering mine. I share these comments with you because I want you to know how important prayer is to me now. I began to notice a few months ago, even in the middle of the night, I'd get up and go to my selected place and pray. It was very comforting and my prayers began to be answered, although I didn't realize it at the time. You are one of those prayers answered.

What I am most pleased with you is your believe in the Word. I didn't know it then, but the person I marry has to try to be and try to do what the Word says. It's clear to me now.

I thank God for bringing you into my life. I'm looking forward to spending the rest of my life with you. I'll keep the wedding vows.

Love,

George

Notable lines from this letter:

1)   "This morning, I asked H if she had been praying, because she is going through some difficult times".
2)   "I began to notice a few months ago, even in the middle of the night, I'd get up and go to my selected place and pray".
3)   "...but the person I marry has to try to be and try to do what the Word says. It's clear to me now".
4)   "I thank God for bringing you into my life. I'm looking forward to spending the rest of my life with you. I'll keep the wedding vows".

In #1 above, H was going through a difficult time because I was sticking to my statement that when our lease was up on September 1, 1994, I was going my separate way.

In item #2, I am noting my commitment to prayer and that prayer has become important to me.

In items 3 &4, I'm speaking marriage and wedding vows.

****

I wrote and faxed this letter on Monday, June 20, 1994

June 20, 1994

My California Sunshine,

Happy Two Week Anniversary! These two weeks brought unexpected joy and satisfaction, and I thank you for that.

These two weeks have given me a great appreciation of the bible and prayer. The Complete Book of Bible Literacy has increased my knowledge and understanding of events and people in the bible. My belief in prayer and expecting what I pray for has never been greater. I've sat back and examined where I am in life and where I want to be. I've prayed on where I want to be and I truly expect to be there one day. You are one of the places I've prayed on being, and I expect to be there one day.

Bertha, you are one of the finest women I've ever met in my life, and I was blessed the day I met you. I know that you are a gift from above.

Love,

GT

Notable lines from this letter:

1)   "Happy Two Week Anniversary! These two weeks brought unexpected joy and satisfaction, and I thank you for that.
2)   The remainder of the letter!

Each time I read these letters, which usually is a few days before our wedding anniversary, and at this point, as I writing now, I'm always struck by the swiftness of how Bertha and I got to this point in our "relationship". If you take a look at the dates up to now, Bertha and I have known each other for three weeks! One week in each others presence, and two weeks long distance. This swiftness was orchestrated by the Holy Spirit! Wow!

****

Bertha faxed me this letter on June 20, 1994

June 20, 1994

George,

I love your conversations. I also love your faxes. You think you will get me to tell you all of my thoughts? I don't think so ... You remind me of a time in my life when I believed I would be totally out of control, because of my feelings for someone, because I felt so close to that person. It happened to have been a Latino Preacher, with whom I had the only relationship of true love I believed I could have.

The Church I was attending at the time did not think it was a good idea for the two of us to be together, so they did all they could to discourage this relationship, which may not have been ideal; Yet we were very much in tune with each other. The only reason I bring this up is because this gentleman knew my every thought. He wanted to know and I knew his. This was the reason he and I were SO close.

Which brings us to George and Bertha. They seem to be starting off the same way. It's awesome in a loving way, and it's dangerous if the relationship will not be sustained. We need to know some very definite things, George. Will we be or not be?

There are many obstacles in our way on your part. If it were my part alone, we would be together tomorrow, in the Loving relationship I believe everyone deserves.

The only thing I can do is wait for you to get your life in order, and I don't think I will wait too long. It is not worth the time because I really am on someone else's territory. I do not intend to intrude, as I want the same seeds I sow to grow in my own life. While you think you need me in your life, high on my priority list is a man living for God first. Therefore, you need to find a Word Oriented Church, because this is more important to me than sex, love, children, money and any other things life has to offer. The loving and affections are easy if the proper priority is placed in the spiritual sense. I've gotta go. More later.

Bertha

Notable lines from this letter:

1)   "Will we be or not be? There are many obstacles in our way on your part".

2)   "The only thing I can do is wait for you to get your life in order, and I don't think I will wait too long. It is not worth the time because I really am on someone else's territory. I do not intend to intrude, as I want the same seeds I sow to grow in my own life".

3)   "While you think you need me in your life, high on my priority list is a man living for God first. Therefore, you need to find a Word Oriented Church, because this is more important to me than sex, love, children, money and any other things life has to offer. The loving and affections are easy if the proper priority is placed in the spiritual sense".

Item 1 and 2 above clearly relate to H. Item 3, a Word Oriented Church, will play a critical role on my journey to May 6, 1995. The greatest change in my life will center on a Word Oriented Church. More on that later.

****

I faxed this letter on June 21, 1994

June 21, 1994

Honey Dearest,

I'm excited about you coming to Philadelphia in December. I've already begun to put together an "itinerary." Philadelphia is a great city! It will be fun planning your stay, choosing where we'll go and what we'll see. Some things we may do may be the first time I do them also. I'll probably have a surprise for you. It will be exciting! Hopefully, you'll return to LA and tell your family and friends that you had a great time in Philadelphia.

To reduce the cost of your visit, I'd like you to stay with me, rather then stay at a hotel. I realize the importance of "waiting", and that's ok with me. If you feel you can't "handle" us being together like that, I'll try to find a friend to stay with.

Our conversation this morning was the finest we've had. I really enjoyed it! I like the idea of a relationship where I put you first and you put me first, that way we're both first in our relationship, second only to God. I know we can have that relationship.

Love,
George

Notable lines from this letter:

1)   "I'm excited about you coming to Philadelphia in December."

2)   "To reduce the cost of your visit, I'd like you to stay with me, rather then stay at a hotel. I realize the importance of "waiting", and that's OK with me. If you feel you can't "handle" us being together like that, I'll try to find a friend to stay with".

3)   "I like the idea of a relationship where I put you first and you put me first, that way we're both first in our relationship, second only to God".

Since Monday, June 6th, I had been talking on the phone (from work) to Bertha almost every morning at 11AM EST, 8AM PST. My plan was to talk no longer than 15 minutes each day, but the time varied from 15 to 60 minutes. As you can imagine, I couldn't talk from home. I need to mention that at this point, Bertha and I had talked about my being on my own as of September 1st, and she believed me.

So, it was very exciting that she agreed to come to Philadelphia from Los Angeles in December. However, I was absolutely determined not to have sex with her. You see, I wanted to do marriage "right" this time, and I was willing to stay with a friend to ease her concerns.

As you should have noted so far, God and the order of marriage has come up many times in our talks, thus the thought of me putting her first and she putting me first was very important in our relationship.

****

I faxed this letter on June 22, 1994

A Poem for

My California Sunshine

It's a beautiful morning in Philadelphia today, and it makes me think of You.

Blue sky, sun, and warmth are You.

You are my sun and my moon, and You are always present.

The clouds during the day and night may hide You, but I know You are always there.

> Written by Your Diamond in the ruff,
> George

Notable lines from this letter:

The whole letter was notable because I had never written a poem before. I was a poet and didn't know it!

****

Bertha faxed me this letter June 23, 1994:

FRAZIER FINANCIAL
P.O. BOX 7514 * CULVER CITY, CA 90233-7514
(213) 295-2034

June 23, 1994

Dearest GT,

It is now 9:50 PM. I sent you an Amvox this afternoon, when I was missing you so terribly. I still am kind of in a mood that I don't like to be in. Of course, it is the end of that time of the month, but usually, that does not bother me. I just feel the need to be near you. It feels like something is missing. I am going to surprise you with something in the mail, my budding Poet.

GT, what's going to happen? As if you know. As my husband, you are supposed to know everything, right? Then tell me Honey, what's going to happen. I don't know, and I feel lost right now. It is such a beautiful night. The moon is full and the air is just right. Not too cool. A night to walk hand and hand, look into each others eyes and feel the mood, then discuss our future. We could walk up the hill, which takes about 40 minutes. When we came back we would be ready to make mad passionate love; Thank God for our families, businesses and other friends in our lives, talk some more and fall asleep in each other's arms That's what I feel like tonight GT. Sleep tight my love.

Your Wife,

Bertha

Notable lines from this letter:

1)   "GT, what's going to happen? As if you know. As my

husband, you are supposed to know everything, right? Then tell me Honey, what's going to happen. I don't know, and I feel lost right now".

2)   "Your Wife Bertha"

This letter is dated 17 days after I returned to Philadelphia and Bertha returned to Los Angeles. Yet, we are already "married" and making "mad passionate love". I'm always amazed each time I read these letters how fast the Holy Spirit was moving in our lives. The movement was so unusual, it just felt like you were being lead along and I in particular, was not asking any questions. It seemed like I was just along for the ride. This was and still is a ride I never experienced before, and have yet to experience it again.

****

I faxed this letter to Bertha on July 1, 1994:

July 1, 1994

My California Sunshine,

It's a beautiful morning in Philadelphia! The day will be sunny, warm, and full of promise, just like you. I received the four books you sent me today. I relate the beautiful day and the books as a sign of a tremendous and exciting future. That future is all wrapped up in you.

I don't know what God has in store for me, but if He gave me my choice, I'd be a very successful businessman who would joyfully relate my happiness, success, and wealth to prayer and faith. After all, I'd have first hand knowledge. I know I'd be effective in getting the message across.

I love you Bertha, and I thank God for you. I believe that through these books, you and He have taken the first steps in turning this piece of coal into a beautiful diamond.

Love,

GT

Notable lines from this letter:
1) "I received the four books you sent me today".
2) "I love you Bertha, and I thank God for you. I believe that through these books, you and He have taken the first steps in turning this piece of coal into a beautiful diamond".

The first notable line is noteworthy because Bertha was feeding my starved human spirit with the books she sent me. I was hungry for God's Word and was very surprised at my reaction to His word. I clearly remember telling Bertha "this stuff sticks", referring to the books. The first book to really capture my attention was "The Complete Book of Bible Literacy". It gave me a tantalizing summary of the bible and I read through it (367 pages) rather quickly. Of the four books Bertha sent me, a book called "If Satan Can't Steal Your Joy He Can't Keep Your Goods" by Jerry Savelle, was the first book I every read that explained how Satan impacts your life.

The second set of lines were noteworthy because even at that juncture in my "relationship" with Bertha, I'm giving God all the credit for where I am and what I'm feeling in my life at that moment.

****

I faxed this letter to Bertha on July 6, 1994:

July 6, 1994

Dear Bertha,

When I was at Virginia Beach I thought of us being there. I'm looking forward to walking the beaches of the world with you, happy in the knowledge that God has given us to each other. When I get to LA in September, I'm looking forward to walking along the beach, hand in hand with you. I've never seen a California sunset. I'm looking forward to it.

Love,

Your Husband, George

****

This letter was faxed to Bertha on July 7, 1994

July 7, 1994

Dear Bertha,

I really enjoyed our conversation yesterday afternoon. I know I can be all that you want me to be, and more. I also know that we will never have a communication problem. I'll try to support you in whatever you do, as I'm sure you'll try to support me. I like how you view the privacy of our home and I share your thoughts.

Our conversation this morning has left me shaking my head in wonderment of what we have. I can't thank God enough for what we will share. I believe one way to thank him is for us to be all that we can be and give him the praise in the presence of others.

I love you so, so much!

George

****

Bertha faxed me this letter on July 11, 1994:

July 11, 1994

George R. Toulson, Sr.

My Dearest Darling,

This letter may be somewhat confusing to you, but bear with me. I have again re-thought my position, and predicament. First off, I will not be unequally yoked with an unbeliever. If we are not at the same level of Christian belief, this situation exists.

Secondly, you have not mentioned your drinking habits with me, even though you know this is crucial, with me. I have been through that before. I know that silence in that regard means. BL was a hopeless alcoholic until I left him for that reason. He is better now, but alcoholics do things which are mind boggling. They kill love quickly. What's worse, I cannot stand to smell alcohol on someone's breath. Kissing is dead.

Church attendance is number one on my list of things to do. I love it! I refuse to force that on anybody. But this is the only way you come to knowledge of faith. You must hear the word, not simply read it. "Faith comes by Hearing". This is not something I can teach you, nor is it my job. As a man, you should teach me. Or else, you lose your position of authority in the home.

Despite your talk of what you have done to educate your children, there is a large grey area in your relationship with R, which causes me great concern. All these things have to be reconciled.

Finally, you were right in the beginning. As a man, you should come to me first. For the years you have not been with R, you should be much better off financially. I don't know that there is a gigantic problem, but something is wrong. I will take no part in restoring anyone to financial security. They must already be there.

I will not spend money to come to Virginia Beach, when I know our relationship as husband and wife is hopeless. If this is of God, which I now doubt, it will still come to fruition. So let the timetable go as you suggested initially, but I do not believe I should get my hopes up high. The real issue with you is financial prosperity, which is OK, but not by itself. It is an outgrowth of being submitted to the Word.

DO NOT TRASH THIS LETTER. KEY ISSUES!

****

Notable lines from this letter:

1) This letter may be somewhat confusing to you, but bear with me. I have again re-thought my position, and predicament. First off, I will not be unequally yoked with an unbeliever. If we are not at the same level of Christian belief, this situation exists.

Bertha is having second thoughts about marriage to me, which I quickly understood. The relationship we're in is nearing 5 weeks old, and based on what you've previously read, we've covered a lot of ground! She doesn't know if I'm a believer, but I sure sound like one! Also, and obviously very important to her, she doesn't know the level of my Christian belief, as evidenced by how I'm living my life. After nearly 5 weeks, I have no evidence!

2) Secondly, you have not mentioned your drinking habits with me, even though you know this is crucial, with me.

At the time (after 7 weeks), the thought of my drinking and it bothering Bertha, hadn't really occurred to me. I was totally caught up on Bertha and what God was doing in my life. I was having the most exciting time of my life.

3) I will not spend money to come to Virginia Beach, when I know our relationship as husband and wife is hopeless. If this is of God, which I now doubt, it will still come to fruition.

"Hopeless" and "doubt"! I could understand where she was coming from, but I had "hope" and there was "no doubt" in my mind about us! Bertha needed to take a deep breath and relax. I knew God was in control. In the next letter to her, I'm trying to help her "lighten up" a bit.

****

This letter faxed to Bertha on July 12, 1994:

July 12, 1994

My California Sunshine,

Here is something to make you smile, laugh, and get those "juices" flowing. The italicized comments are my own.

* A good man is hard to find – and hard to keep good.

(I'll be good, very good!)

* A hard man is good to find.

(That's me Baby!)

* A woman has to have a bad man once or twice in her life to be thankful for a good one.

(I'm a real good one!)

* Embryologically speaking, is it correct to say that the penis is an exaggerated clitoris?

(Intellectually stimulating)

* Why is a clitoris like Antarctica?

- Because men know its down there, but how many really care?

(I care a lot!)

* Man has his will – but woman has her way.

(Sad, but true)

* What's the worst thing about oral sex?

_- The view

(I disagree)

What do you call a woman who can suck a golf ball through fifty feet of garden hose?

- Darling

(Yes, Yes, Yes!!!)

Love You Baby,

GT

****

Notable lines from this letter:

"Here is something to make you smile, laugh, and get those "juices" flowing. The italicized comments are my own".

Remember the previous letter Bertha faxed to me was one of hopelessness and doubt? I was trying to really change the subject. I succeeded!

****

I faxed this letter on July 14, 1994:

My Thoughts at The Time

It's 11:15PM EST, July 14, 1994

I'm restless. You are on my mind.

I'm lonely.

I want to go out.

But I've had a couple of drinks and I'm not driving the car.

I could walk and get a beer or two.

But do I want to? No.

What I want to do is something which I can't do now.

I want to be in a loving conversation with you.

Dreaming of what we'll do tomorrow, next week, next month, next year, and the next 5 years.

That's what I want.

I'm listening to some smooth jazz. Feels nice.

Just like you will, Mrs. Toulson.

Love,

Your Husband

****

Notable lines from this letter:

I would rather have you the reader, relating to what I'm feeling as I wrote this letter, but as I read over the letter, this line has a day of reckoning in the future.

"I could walk and get a beer or two".

In the previous letter from Bertha, she made it clear she had a major problem with alcohol. In my letter, the alcohol problem wasn't registering.

****

I faxed this letter to Bertha on July 15, 1994

July 15, 1004

Good morning, my California Sunshine,

At 4am this morning, I was wide awake and you were occupying all my thoughts. I'm still somewhat amazed at the speed and clarity of those thoughts. Everything was positive and creative. It was awesome! So what am I talking about? I'm talking about our future!

I'd like to be in a position to come to Los Angeles in late September and discuss my thoughts and yours, face to face. One of the things I'll want to discuss with you is my financial status and my plan to get out of debt. I'd like to stay a week. Jack said I could stay with him and his family.

It feels so good to feel the way I do about us. There are some challenges, but what is life without challenges?

Your Pennsylvania Peach,
George

****

I hope this letter conveys to you how truly happy I was at this point. Whenever I'd sit down to write something to Bertha, the thoughts were so clear and it never took me long to convey my thoughts. Wait 'til you read the next fax, entitled "The Vision". You'd have to hire someone to help you miss this one!

****

I faxed this letter to Bertha on July 15, 1994

The Vision

The wedding is relatively small. The reception however, is much larger. It's a time of celebration. After the greetings and introductions are made, the garter is off your thigh, we've done some dancing, said thank you and goodbye to our friends, we're off.

We are in our honeymoon suite. We embrace gently, for we are relieved the wedding and the reception are past us. We walk out on the balcony and look at something majestic. We're quiet for a moment because, we realize that this is our beginning.

We freshen up and both of us are attired in something appropriate. We order something light from room service just to give us an excuse to stay attired for a while, savoring the expectation.

Then, it's time ...

You go into the bathroom to refresh what you initially freshened up. I'm in the bed, waiting for you. You approach the bed slowly. A few feet from the bed, you stop and let what you're wearing slip off.

To your body, my lips and fingers are like lighting jolts! To me, your body is a priceless treasure. I look at you, touch you, smell you, hear you, and taste you. I'm hot, ... but I'm cool. For I have to "take you places" you haven't been in awhile, and for that, I must be gentle, slow, and deliberate.

It is wonderful ...

Later, you awaken. You reach out your hand and touch me, for I am there.

I love you,

George

****

Wow!!! I was a poet and now I know it!

CHAPTER 4
GOD'S GRACE

At this point in the story, Bertha and I have been communicating (talking on the phone, faxes, and post cards) for about 5 weeks. This was all about to change. How many of you forgot that I was still living with H? On Saturday, July 16th, Bertha called me at home. She just wanted to talk with me, rather than wait until Monday. However, in my speaking with her, she heard H's voice in the background. Reality hit hard and she hung up. When I called her Monday morning, she was upset with me and herself. I told her that my plan was still moving forward, in that I would be moving to my own place as of September 1st. Her response to me was "...if you get your act together, call me around September 1st and we'll see where we stand...". Shortly after this time, perhaps 2 weeks, I received at work a letter size manila envelope. There was no return address, although the post mark said Los Angeles, CA. Inside the manila envelope were all the faxes and post cards I ever sent to Bertha! In looking at the address on the manila envelope, my name was not on the envelope. The envelope just read "CoreState Bank, 1500 Market St, Phila, PA 19103. Someone, probably in the CoreStates mailroom, had opened the envelope to see who this mail belonged to. I wonder how much they read. In any case, it got to me. It took me awhile to grasp the significance of receiving the faxes and postcards back, but I immediately thanked God for bringing them safely to me. For without them, I wouldn't be writing this story now. Plus, later on, I used them to make a point to you know who.

Bertha - Surprise, Surprise

It was about July when I began to feel such a void when I did not talk to GT on the week-end. The number he gave me did not work on the week-end. I had to use the AmVox line and it was not like hearing his voice live. I suspected he might be living with someone, but I was certain he told me he was not married and did not have a girlfriend.

Up to this point, all the talking at work and in the evening was working. But I still felt lost on the week-end. I was very emotionally tied into him by now. So I voiced my concern about not being able to reach him on the week-end. The butterflies in my stomach and the emotions in my head worked overtime. I felt my womanhood operating strongly. So I told him how I was feeling and he gave me a number and time to call that Saturday. So I called.

George started in on the sweet talk about us, our love, and probable marriage. I spoke back to him with the passion only a woman in love could express. All of a sudden, I heard someone in a loud voice say something. I could not tell if it was a woman or man because the voice had a deep pitch. George said, "I'll call you back". Talk about cold water on those hot passions! He didn't call me back until Monday.

Once I found out it was a woman he had been living with for more than 6 years, I told him to get lost and don't send me anything - card, letter, teddy bear or nothing. I was through. Just that fast, I shut down. George said they had discussed him going on his way when the lease was up in August. To that I said, "don't call me until you get yourself together".

I did not hear from George for the balance of July or in August, and when September came, I knew he did not know my birthday, but I had already said to MQ in the office, if he has not called me by September 7 (my birthday) at 8AM, he is history. This was a fleece. Also, this was a way of proving that George was a deception and counterfeit of the real thing. I did everything I could to test God and George. I thought I would feel good when I could close the door and say that was deception. Believing it was the real thing was more uncomfortable.

On September 7th , I came to work beaming and I said to MQ, "I told you he was not the one. I knew everything was just too good to be true". Here it is, about 11AM, and I had not heard a word. Then my spirit said, "call home for messages". I called home and I could not believe my ears. George had called at 8:01 EST. In the message he left was these words, "here is my new address and my home phone number, let's move forward". I was shaking and MQ was smiling. Where can I go to hide my tears.

George – Game Time

After the H encounter, I had approximately 6 weeks to get my act together. The one thing I knew was I needed to move to Philadelphia. To be honest, I didn't have the extra money required for a security deposit, the first month's rent and furniture, as I was still paying child support for a son still in college, but I was driven to move forward. What I also didn't know was that I was about to enter into God's Grace.

In talking with a friend of mine FE, he was looking to move from the suburbs of West Chester to Philadelphia also. He suggested we look in the Chestnut Hill section of Philadelphia and we began to look for a townhome to rent, which we quickly found. We agreed that the townhome would be in my name and that he would put up the earnest deposit and buy all the furniture, and we would split the rent fifty-fifty. I'd pay for all the utilities. We accomplished this in one week's time! I didn't know it at the time, but that was God's Grace (unmerited favor) working in my life!

Towards the end of August, some friends of mine helped me move from West Chester, PA to the Chestnut Hill section of Philadelphia. I was in my new townhome on September 1st , as I told Bertha I would be. It took a few days for the furniture to arrive and I was away at an AMWAY function out of state for a few days.

On September 7, 1994, I called Bertha in Los Angeles at a few minutes before 11AM EST. The words I spoke to her initially were brief. I said, "I moved into my new townhome. Let's move forward". What I didn't know was that day was her birthday, and she had told her co-worker that if I didn't call by

11AM PST on September 7th , she was walking away from me, from us. She never told me there was a deadline, but God knew. He made sure I called a few minutes before her 11AM deadline. God's Grace again. I've learned that God will show up. Even if it's the 11th hour, 59th minute, and 59th second! God is faithful! Bertha and I moved FORWARD!

A New Season in My Life

Having my own place after 6 years of living with someone else was new and exciting. Couple that with a new found joy in the Lord, my future wife, and marriage, I was pretty happy! Looking back on that season of my life, I noticed that I didn't have a plan. Bertha and I weren't engaged, and we didn't know where we were going to live. Was she going to come live with me in Philadelphia (after we were married), or was I going to live with her in Los Angeles? Looking back, I believe that I was being guided by the Holy Spirit. I'm fond of saying. "I had blinders on". The purpose of having blinders on a horse is so the horse won't be distracted. There were plenty of opportunities for me to be distracted. I had a new townhome with a fireplace, new furniture and finished basement. The way the townhome was furnished, there was plenty of ambience. There were women that would have enjoyed coming to visit me. But that never happened. The most exciting part of my day was talking to Bertha, usually after 8PM (the phone rates were lower). One situation did come into play on my decision as to where to live. In September 1994 CoreStates, my employer, announced that in March of 1995, layoffs would occur for the first time in the company's history. There would be a severance package available, but further details would be forthcoming as March 1995 approached. I knew I'd take the package. As you read, there will be many instances where things just fell into place, both in my life and Bertha's life as our wedding date of May 6, 1995 approached. The only answer I have is we both were guided by the Holy Spirit!

26 ½ Hours - Bertha

We began to plan for a trip to meet. I was going to Washington, DC for the Congressional Black Caucus function held every year in D.C. George said he would come in from Philadelphia to meet me. This would be the first time we had seen each other since June, and it is now mid September. When I got to D.C., I could not wait to see him. I set another fleece out. Saying I know he was money strapped, but if I could get to DC from California, he had better be able to get there from Philadelphia, or we would not continue.

GT had a friend who was coming to DC, so he caught a ride. We stayed together in my hotel room. Went out into the marketplace and bought snacks for the room and saw the folks at the Caucus. What a good time we had. We were so passionate, but no sex. From all indications, we were going to be very compatible. When we went to sleep, I felt so comfortable with George, I did not want to wake up. I liked the way we snuggled.

It was my idea for us to take a train to Philadelphia so I could see George's townhome. It was September and warm, but I brought long coats and wintery stuff. I left my clothes at the hotel while we went to Philly. We took the train from DC and went to Philadelphia. We got cheesesteak sandwiches at Pat's and Geno's. I took photos of everything I could. George's townhome was sweet. It had 4 stories, including a basement where he set up his office. We spent 26 ½ hours together. Then it was time for me to leave and go back to DC (Without George - Not Good). At the train station, George gave me instructions about what to do and not do. He told me to keep my "walkman" on and don't go to sleep. When the train pulls out, the tears began to flow. I looked around to see if anybody was looking and I cried as George got farther and farther away. What a lonesome feeling of only a couple of minutes, but it lasted until I got to DC I followed George's detailed instructions. At last the taxi to the hotel got me there in good time. Opening the door to the hotel room where we had spent so many joy filled hours, the reality hit me. I was leaving first thing in the morning, returning to Los Angeles, and George would not be with me. I called George as soon as I got into the hotel room, and we talked until I was sleepy. Good night, Sweetheart.

26 ½ Hours - George

Up until now, Bertha and I have only seen each other one time. Can you believe that? Well, here comes the second time. Each year in September, the Congressional Black Caucus, African American members of Congress, have their annual event in Washington, DC, and Bertha decided to come east to the event. She arrived on a Thursday and was staying at a downtown hotel. A friend of mine just happened to be driving down to Washington on Friday and I caught a ride with him. It was exciting riding down to see her. When she opened the door, it was a WOW moment! She had on "daisy dukes" and she was looking good! I got my second, third, fourth kiss, probably more! Remember, the first kiss was at the Orlando Airport in June, where she thought she would never see me again?

At the time, I knew Bertha was older than me, but I didn't mention it. A few months later, Bertha's daughter Felicia would "let it slip" that her Mom was born in 1941, making her 9 years older than me. Obliviously, that didn't matter.

I don't even remember if we went out to dinner. What I remember was there were twin beds. I have to admit, there were thoughts crossing my mine, but I suppressed them. I slept on one twin and she slept on the other. The next morning, Saturday, we got dressed up and went to the annual Prayer Breakfast sponsored by the Congressional Black Caucus. After the prayer breakfast, Bertha asked if she could visit my townhome, so we took the Amtrak train to Philadelphia. Since she was leaving early Sunday morning to go back to Los Angeles, me going back to Philadelphia that Saturday afternoon worked out perfectly. Bertha later said the reason she came to visit my townhome was to check to see if there were any women's belongings at the house, of which there weren't. After the visit, we boarded the R7 train to 30th Street Station in Philadelphia, where she would catch Amtrak back to DC. While we waited for the train, I pulled out the manila envelope with all the faxes and post cards that she mailed back to me in a fit of emotional distress. I read each and every letter that I included in this writing, along with all of the postcards I sent her. Bertha started crying with the first letter and didn't stop until everything was read. Payback!!! I then said to her that me receiving the manila envelope, without my name on it, and no return address, was evidence that God was somehow involved in us being together, which you the reader can see is true, else this writing probably would not be taking place. All together, Bertha and I spent 26 ½ hours together from the time I met her in DC to her leaving me in Philadelphia going back to DC.

Creative Word of Faith Church

The timeframe now is the beginning of October. Bertha strongly suggested that I needed a "Word teaching" ministry. This type of ministry focuses on teaching an individual what the Word of God (the Bible) says about the three-fold God-head – God the Father, God the Son, and God the Holy Spirit. Some ministries/religions won't teach about the Holy Spirit and some very rarely mention Jesus Christ. For many years Bertha attended Crenshaw Christian Center Church in Los Angeles, CA. This is the church that Dr. Fredrick K. C. Price founded in 1973 and the church structure, the physical building, is known throughout the world as the "Faithdome". Dr. Price also founded the Fellowship of Inter-City Word of Faith Ministries (FICWFM), which comprises inter-city churches from all regions of the USA. In Bertha's search for a church for me, she contacted a friend at Crenshaw Christian Center and asked if there were any FICWFM churches in Philadelphia. There were two churches and I intended to visit both of them. At the time, I was living in the Chestnut Hill section of Philadelphia, which was located in the outer fringes of northwest Philadelphia. Creative Word of Faith Church was in the southeast corner of Philadelphia. I had just moved to Philadelphia and I didn't have a car. So the first Sunday I went to Creative Word of Faith. I took the R7 train from Chestnut Hill to Center City Philadelphia, where I got on the Broad Street Subway going south. I got off the subway at Morris St., which was essentially 14th and Morris. I then had to walk 8 blocks to 6th & Morris.

Upon arriving at 6th & Morris around 11AM, I noticed a small crowd of people standing outside of the church. I walked up to a gentleman and introduced myself. That gentleman introduced himself as Pastor Charles Waters. He said the church was experiencing an electrical problem. I don't recall exactly how long we were standing outside, perhaps 20 minutes, but in those 20 minutes, he ministered to me like no man had ever before and I knew I liked this man. I enjoyed the church service and got a chance to meet everyone in the church. The service was over about 1PM or so. I then started the trek back to Chestnut Hill. For whatever reasons, probably because of the R7 Sunday train schedule, I didn't get home until 4PM. I said to myself, "I can't do this each Sunday. I'll go to the second church next Sunday". It never happened. I was back at Creative Word of Faith at 11AM, and didn't get home until 3-4PM that Sunday, and for most of the Sundays in the future.

My friend FE bought me The Original African Heritage Study Bible (King James Version) and he gave it to me on October 14, 1994. It was copywrited in 1993 by The James C. Winston Publishing Company. I will be forever grateful to him, for this bible is the most important and most interesting book I've ever read. Earlier in this writing, I mentioned that there were several biblical related books that Bertha sent me. In those books were many scriptural references that now I could reference in my new bible. I remember the very first passage in the bible I yellow highlighted. It was Mark chapter 4. It reads, 1 And he began again to teach by the sea side: and there was gathered unto him a great multitude, so that he entered into a ship, and sat in the sea; and the whole multitude was by the sea on the land. 2 And he taught them many things by parables, and said unto them in his doctrine, 3 Hearken; Behold, there went out a sower to sow: 4 And it came to pass, as he sowed, some fell by the way side, and the fowls of the air came and devoured it up. 5 And some fell on stony ground, where it had not much earth; and immediately it sprang up, because it had no depth of earth: 6 But when the sun was up, it was scorched; and because it had no root, it withered away. 7 And some fell among thorns, and the thorns grew up, and choked it, and it yielded no fruit. 8 And other fell on good ground, and did yield fruit that sprang up and increased; and brought forth, some thirty, and some sixty, and some an hundred. 9 And he said unto them, He that hath ears to hear, let him hear. 10 And when he was alone, they that were about him with the twelve asked of him the parable. 11 And he said unto them, Unto you it is given to know the mystery of the kingdom of God: but unto them that are without, all these things are done in parables: 12 That seeing they may see, and not perceive; and hearing they may hear, and not understand; lest at any time they should be converted, and their sins should be forgiven them. 13 And he said unto them, Know ye not this parable? and how then will ye know all parables? 14 The sower soweth the word. 15 And these are they by the way side, where the word is sown; but when they have heard, Satan cometh immediately, and taketh away the word that was sown in their hearts. 16 And these are they likewise which are sown on stony ground; who, when they have heard the word, immediately receive it with gladness; 17 And have no root in themselves, and so endure but for a time: afterward, when affliction or persecution ariseth for the word's sake, immediately they are offended. 18 And these are they which are sown among thorns; such as hear the word, 19 And the cares of this world, and the deceitfulness of riches, and the lusts of other things entering in, choke the word, and it becometh unfruitful. 20 And these are they which are sown on good ground; such as hear the word, and receive it, and bring forth fruit, some thirtyfold, some sixty, and some an hundred.

Beginning in verse 14, everyone who has ever desired to know the Word of God falls into one the four categories of a believer. The first category of believers is in verse 15. The second category of believers are in verses 16 and 17. The third category of believers are in verses 18 and 19. The fourth and final category is in verse 20. I fell into the third category. This and other revelations made me want to know more and more of what the Word of God says. I took pride in taking my bible to Creative Word of Faith Church each Sunday.

Everything the Word of God (the bible) said was essentially new to me, and Pastor Waters taught the Word in an enjoyable and understanding style. One teaching he taught me has stayed with me to this day. A spirit–filled believer (I'll cover what that means later) has to be able to say, "I will not be moved by how I feel or don't feel, I will not be moved by what I see or don't see, I will not be moved by what I hear or don't hear. I am only moved by the Spirit of the Living God (the Holy Spirit)". Let that sink in for a moment. When you are hurting physically, can your human spirit rise up and command your mouth to say, I will not be moved by how I feel or don't feel? When you see something you wish you didn't see or you were expecting to see something, but it didn't appear, can your human spirit rise up and command your mouth to say, I will not be moved by what I see or don't see? When you hear something you didn't want to hear, or you were expecting to hear something that you didn't hear, can your human spirit rise up and command your mouth to say, I will not be moved by what I hear or don't hear? When your mouth can speak to the issue at hand, you are walking by faith and not by sight!

I was like a sponge every Sunday at Creative Word of Faith, and I enjoyed talking to Bertha every Sunday, reviewing what Pastor Waters had taught that Sunday. I was being fed the Word!

Bertha & I Getting Ahead of Ourselves

Bertha

Passions were flying hot and heavy from communications with George. They were getting to such a pitch, that I knew something had to happen. There was a high powered conference being held in Honolulu, HI, so I was going. The thought came to me, if GT could join me, we could get married there and have our honeymoon. I would be staying for 2 weeks. It was not to be. George could not just leave his job and come. Instead, he had me re-focus my thinking and look for hotels and venues for a properly pre-planned wedding. That's what I did. I interviewed hotels and priced wedding packages. I went shopping and found a music audio tape of wedding songs. This was in November. I talked to George during the day and night. With the romantic atmosphere of Hawaii, I spent my time musing, even in the conference, where all the mucky mucks in community development and micro lending were in attendance.

CHAPTER 5
CHRISTMAS

George
It's now November and marriage and a wedding date is the predominate part of our phone conversations. Bertha was actually pushing to get married in November, but I wasn't feeling that. We agreed that she would go to Hawaii and do reconnaissance and report back. What she brought back, and I was agreeable to was, we were honeymooning in Hawaii and music to use at the wedding.

Merry Christmas - George

We decided that Bertha would spend Christmas with me. She would arrive on December 17th and leave on January 1, 1995. When Bertha arrived, she had at least 4 large pieces of luggage. She said she didn't know if we were going to get married then or not, so she brought clothes and stuff in the event that we got married and we decided she was going to live in Philadelphia. She even brought the wedding rings! She came prepared! We went to my doctor and took blood tests and went to City Hall in Philadelphia and purchased a marriage license. Bertha found her wedding dress and veil at a consignment store in Chestnut Hill, not very far from my townhome. We went to Creative Word of Faith and talked with Pastor Waters, and we decided to get married at the church the Sunday after Christmas.

Bertha and I slept together but there was no sex. Even with the ambiance of the townhouse, especially the wood burning fireplace, I had decided that we'd limit our kissing and touching so that things wouldn't go too far. I was determined that I would do the pre-marriage things right this time, in every way I knew how. However, there was one particular time when all it would have taken way a slight movement on my part and penetration would have occurred. Two people couldn't have been any closer than we were. I remember saying to Bertha, I want to wait until our marriage night. I want to do it God's way. As I look back, this was not difficult because the Holy Spirit was guiding us. I wanted to be obedient to God. To this day, our sex is still vibrant, and I thank God every day for our sweet and tender love making. I believe our not having sex before we were married is what is blessing our love making now.

Soon after Bertha arrived, we went out and bought our first Christmas tree together. Since we didn't have a car, we walked home carrying the tree together. We put up the tree, decorated it and decorated the townhome, and invited our family to have Christmas dinner with us. We invited my Mom and Dad, my sons and daughters - Demetria, Angie, George, and Charles. Bertha also invited Felicia, her daughter, who was living just outside of Washington, DC. No one knew what to expect and no one was surprised that Bertha was there. After dinner, we made the announcement of our engagement. Everyone was totally surprised and wanted to know how this happened! We didn't mention where we were going to live because we really didn't know. Once I mentioned that Bertha was from Los Angeles, Angie said she knew that I would be moving to Los Angeles, which proved correct.

Merry Christmas - Bertha

It was December when I came to visit George in Philadelphia for the last time. He had decided that he would leave and go to a friend's house, so that we would not be tempted to have sex before our marriage. At first, I had suggested I stay at a Holiday Inn in downtown Philadelphia. The commute would be cumbersome in that George did not have a car. So we agreed and George was committed to stay away from engaging in sexual intercourse while I was in his townhome. I was afraid because now I am seeing him up close and personal. I did not know what this situation would present. What I did know is that I had received an audible Word from The Lord, that the next time I had intercourse, it had better be with my Husband.

In view of the above, I had bought wedding bands, in case we could not contain ourselves. We enjoyed each other's company, and I did attend his multi-level marketing meeting with Amway the night I arrived. After a long day flying, and now a business meeting which lasted hours, I made it through. Donna, a colleague of George's picked us up from his townhome and we all went to the meeting, held at a hotel near the Philadelphia International Airport. I could visualize how our lives could come together as partners in business. Multi-level marketing had been my side job for years. I worked in "Shapefast", selling health care and dietary supplements. After the meeting, we went to a local restaurant. Donna and I ate salads, while George went through his presentation. When he was done, I had to get him another salad because somehow, we ate his too. I knew he was "cash strapped", but I was "rolling in dough", as his equal opposite.

Once back at the townhome, we showered and went to bed. I loved listening to the radio station (WDAS-FM) and the moon shone in his window as it had done in my bedroom in LA. We talked and kissed and fell asleep. What a chance we were taking. George seemed more determined than I to keep celibate. I would not advise this arrangement to anyone. It is peculiar how he had such restraint – given his history with women. But, we made it. We had plans to get with Donna the next day, and also to go to church. We had much to do.

At Creative Word of Faith Church, I met Pastor Waters and his wife Mary, along with the small congregation of loving people in attendance. Boy, it was a long way to church, but I was with George and now talking to the man who demonstrated such commitment to me and to our Lord, as well. We had dinner downstairs in the church, where the congregation brought covered dishes. Wonderful was the fellowship and this family of believers. Pastor Waters had a teaching style of Pastor Price in Los Angeles. He taped his sermons. I felt right at home.

Arriving back at the townhome, George and I continued our discourse, and vowed our love for each other and decided we must get married sooner rather than later. We were taking too much of a chance. So, we found ourselves making schedules of things to do. George went to work on Monday, while I stayed home. I missed him all day long. I did not want to chance going out into the neighborhood until I was sure I would not get lost. So I stayed inside of this beautiful townhome, until George arrived home in the evening. He so much looked like the husband I wanted to live with for the rest of my days. He cooked dinner, we ate and he washed dishes and I was a prima donna. This was a great environment. So I began to plan that since I had always wanted to be on the east coast, we would live here. I needed a job. So George took me into downtown Philly and introduced me to one of his Urban Banker friends while he went to work. I had lunch and just "hung out" in the Gallery until he got off work. We took the train home, and I settled in to wanting to live in Philadelphia.

We had some close encounters of the sex kind. So we got Donna to take us to downtown Philly to get our marriage license. We already had the rings. George had tried on his wedding band and the anointing on it so heavy, he took it off like it was hot! We had gone to George's physician and got blood tests. I brought enough clothes to last for a season. So, I was ready to be Mrs. George Ronald Toulson, Sr. I did not think too much about Pennie back in L.A. Just getting married was all we wanted to do right now. Basically we wanted to consummate our marriage. So we were off and running in a frantic pace to get this done. If I needed to go back to L.A. – fine, just as long as we were married.

We scheduled counseling with Pastor Waters. Our plans were to get married after church on the following Sunday, December 27th, and use the atmosphere of the church dinner downstairs as our wedding reception. We were ready. It would be no problem to wait for Sunday. We had many other things to do.

Christmas Day

We had prepared a big Christmas dinner and invited Mom and Dad, Demetria, Angie, George Jr., Charles, and Felicia. After dinner, after everyone had opened their gifts, George called everyone together. Mind you, this was the first time I had met Mom and Dad and George's young adults. So, the family did not have a clue about what was about to be announced. Realizing these facts, I was a little apprehensive as to what the reaction to me as George's fiancée, would be to the family.

As a matter of fact, before I had descended the stairway to make my initial entrance, Felicia preceded me and stated she was me. I don't know why she would do that but she did. I am sure Mom and Dad thought, what's he done now with this young woman; So, they may have relaxed somewhat when they saw me. The atmosphere was warm and nice and the smell of the turkey and dressing, ham and the fixings (prepared mostly by George) put everybody at ease. A few days previous to this day, we had walked a couple of blocks and found the perfect Christmas tree. George decorated the tree himself. He had his own ideas of what should be placed where. The ornaments were his, and were placed perfectly. The fireplace was going and topped off the atmosphere. Intermittent snow flurries made this scene just right.

Now comes the big announcement. I had strategically placed myself behind George, just in case someone threw a shoe. Straight shouldered and without hesitancy, came the words, Bertha and I are engaged to be married. Everyone was polite. No comments were made, but I heard later that Mom had plenty to say – all negative including a curse word.
The day ended on a positive note. I had brought many souvenir

gifts from Venice Beach. Maybe these were my peace offerings. They were well received.

Donna came over the next day and the three of us walked downtown in Chestnut Hill. Donna and I went into a consignment shop. George went across the street to a computer store. We saw many shopping opportunities. I was having a good time. All of a sudden, I saw a wedding dress on the wall. I asked about it. It was my size. Donna said you had better get that dress, so I did. We hid it from George because this was going back to LA with me. I went back to that same store the day before I left for LA. The store owner said she hoped that I'd come back because she didn't know how to contact me. She said here is the petticoat that goes with that dress. The whole dress came to a total of $50.00. And it is beautiful! This was an unexpected blessing and would prove to be another indication that George and I were on God's timetable.

Wedding Called Off - Bertha

Saturday night, FE came over and brought his girlfriend, and we went to the 2nd Annual Black Professionals Gala in Center City Philadelphia. We had a great time. After we came back to the townhome, while we were all sitting around the fireplace, George had a glass of liquor. He tried to be amorous towards me and his whole demeanor change. I smelled the liquor and looked at him and just became repulsed. "Oh no, not another Billy", I thought. I cannot do this!!!! The more he tried to kiss me, the more turned off I got. My mind raced about the wedding tomorrow. I could not tell George, but I have to tell Pastor Waters.

That Sunday, was a gloomy day in my life. I felt like a traitor. I told Pastor Waters secretly what had happened. He called George and me into an area and there broke the news to George. He said, "Brother George" I cannot marry you and Sister Bert. I have an obligation to do God's will and protect Pastor Price's sheep. George stared out the church window, and I thought I saw tears coming from his eyes. He promised that alcohol would not be a problem, but I knew he had no real control over it. So, we went back to his townhome where we did not speak for the remainder of the day. Felicia was there and knew something was wrong. She remained downstairs with George, and they watched football. I retreated to the bedroom and stayed there. After a couple of hours, I came downstairs just to check the atmosphere then returned upstairs. The second time I came downstairs, George managed to say to me, "I'm on the mend".

CHAPTER 6
GEORGE'S REACTION

I was hurt and disappointed that the wedding didn't take place, or so I thought. I say it this way because now I know that was not what God wanted for us. God wanted the best for us, and us getting married on Sunday, December 27, 1994 was not God's best. I sulked a couple of days, but realized it was best we didn't get married. I began to think about Bertha leaving in a few days, and what would happen after that. We initially decided we would get married towards the end of May. We don't remember why we came up with that date, but Bertha did a calculation and determined her monthly, which she said came like clock-work, would occur toward the end of May, so we decided on the first week-end in May. We further decided to bring in the New Year at Time Square in New York City. We were going to watch the ball drop in person.

We decided to take the train to New York City on December 30th. Prior to leaving, we made hotel reservations and got maps of the city. This was the first time Bertha had ever been to New York City. I hadn't been to New York City since I was 10 years old, so it was my first time too. On New Years Eve, we wore 5 layers of clothing, and we arrived at Time Square about 7PM. It was cold, but we were excited just to be in the crowd. We stood most of the time. We have never been in a crowd of that many people again. We met people from all over the world. At midnight, we hugged and kissed and were amazed at how quickly Time Square emptied after midnight.

We were back on the train going to Philadelphia around 1PM on New Years Day. About half way home, we both got quiet. Bertha would be leaving later that evening. When it was time for Bertha to leave, we decided it would be best for us both that I not go with her to the airport. So, I put her on the shuttle, not knowing when I'd see her again. This was only the third time that I'd seen Bertha. Wow!

17 Weeks

Beginning January 1, 1995, 17 weeks takes us to May 6, 1995, our scheduled wedding date. The first week in January was when the news of our engagement reached my CoreStates Bank colleagues and other Philadelphia associates. None of my colleagues or associates took it seriously, including my townhouse mate, FE. He laughed and gave me a look of disbelief when I told him that there had been no sex with Bertha. I also told him that I was going to remain celibate until marriage. He really laughed at that one. He said if I couldn't be faithful to this one or that one, and I lived with them, how could he believe that I was going to be faithful to someone who lives 3,000 miles away? He had a really good laugh.

The news also reached Bertha's massive Los Angeles family. Bertha came from a family of 10 siblings, 8 girls and 2 boys. At this time, there were only 7 sisters and one brother living. Surprise about the news of Bertha's engagement was truly an understatement regarding her family. No one knew anything about me. When did we meet? Where did we meet? How did we meet? What did I look like? I was the mystery guy! Bertha and I have often said we would have loved to have been a fly on the wall of each sister's, niece's, and nephew's home. The fly on the wall also goes for Bertha's business colleagues. We can imagine that there were some good-hearted laughter and jokes, as well as some not so good-hearted laughter and jokes. One reported comment was that Bertha would be married only at the Marriage Feast of the Lamb. You may have to look that partial scripture up to get the meaning.

One interesting dynamic to the family situation is while Bertha had 7 sisters and one brother, and a host of grown nieces and nephews, I was an only child and all my children, were still in college. One question that Bertha was always asked by her family was where we were going to live? I didn't get many questions.

Seventeen weeks can seem like a long if you're not focused. I was determined to stay focused and take one week at a time. I was talking to Bertha from work and after 8PM everyday. Saturday was my toughest day. The only interaction I had with people was my small AMWAY group. I didn't socialize outside of that group. If we weren't doing anything on Saturday, it was a long day for me being at home alone. My roommate FE was always in and out and occasionally he'd have friends over. I had a VCR at home and I watched a lot of movies. Since I was new to the Chestnut Hill neighborhood, I walked around getting familiar with the area, but I didn't have a car and it was winter time. So, there was only so much walking I'd do. Before Bertha left for Los Angeles, she gave me two Yolanda Adams tapes that I played over and over again. Saturday was the day I spent the most reading the bible. However, I was still drinking. I wanted to believe that drinking was helping me pass the time on Saturday.

Sunday was my best day of the week. I would head out for Creative Word of Faith church around 9AM, usually arriving about 10:45. Our congregation was small, but that didn't matter to me. On some Sundays, we'd have less than 10 people in the service. However, Pastor Waters still preached and taught like there were hundreds in the congregation. I was absorbing his every word from the Word of God. Many times it felt as if he was preaching to and teaching me personally. I felt I was learning about something great and wonderful, God's Word. And the more I learned, the more I wanted to learn more. Especially intriguing to me was praying in the Spirit or praying in tongues. I completely understood the concept and practicality of praying in the Spirit and embraced it fully.

Tuesday was bible study night, from 6:30-8PM. For me, it was a power-packed time of learning and asking questions. Elder Wing, part of the church leadership, would always give me a ride home, and as soon as I'd get home, I'd call Bertha, reviewing what we discussed at bible study.

In the early part of March, I left CoreStates and that, in and of itself, was exciting. I also received a call from the wedding coordinator strongly suggesting that I come to Los Angeles ASAP. Bertha was becoming anxious with all she was trying to accomplish. After all, I'm in Philadelphia and she is in LA putting together the wedding, reception, and honeymoon.

I remember catching the R7 train from Chestnut Hill to Suburban Station in Center City Philadelphia, then getting the Airport Shuttle train to Philadelphia International Airport. I also remember that when I got off the Airport Shuttle Train, it was a very gray and very dreary day. So, I went to Los Angeles for 4 days. I arrived Friday evening and l would leave late Tuesday morning. This would be my first time in Los Angeles. Bertha met me at the airport and it was so good to see her. When we arrived at 3719 Mt. Vernon Dr., overlooking downtown Los Angeles, I knew I was in for something special. The glitter of the lights and the skyline were spectacular.

Pennie, Bertha's step-mother was there to greet me. Bertha actually was staying with Pennie, taking care of her. 3719 Mount Vernon Dr. was Bertha's late father's estate, where Pennie had a life estate in the property. She was very nice and smiled all the time. Bertha said she was happy that a man would be living in the house.

Saturday morning, after riding around LA for a couple of hours, doing a little sight seeing, we went back to the house to work on the following:

1)   selecting the music that would be played at the wedding
2)   discussed the style of the tuxedo I'd wear
3)   determined the number of invitations that would be sent out and what the invitations would say

We left again and:

4)   met with owner of the restaurant where the reception would be held and discussed what food would be served at the reception
5)   met the baker and discussed the type of cake we wanted at the reception
6)   toured the hotel where we'd be staying for our honeymoon
7)   drove to Crenshaw Christian Center Church where we were going to be married in a garden wedding

Later that Saturday, with nothing but sunshine and deep blue sky, we went to Venice Beach to watch my first Los Angeles sunset. That was fantastic!

On Sunday, we went to Crenshaw Christian Center Church. That was an experience, being in the "Faithdome". In fact, I remember in 1994, while living West Chester, PA, I was flipping through channels one Sunday evening. I came to a channel where I saw a pastor walking around a huge facility and it looked round on the inside. What I was looking at was the Faithdome at Crenshaw Christian Center. To be there, while reflecting on what I saw on TV, was pretty cool.

On Monday, we had a pre-marital counseling appointment with Pastor Jimmy Price, who would be marrying us. Pastor Jimmy was the nephew of Dr. Frederick K.C. Price, the founder and pastor of Crenshaw Christian Center Church. The counseling went well and it just added to the already building excitement. Our marriage date was approximately 8 weeks away.

Before I flew out on Tuesday, we walked the neighborhood, which was called View Park. It was called View Park because it had a high elevation, such that you could actually look down on downtown LA. View Park also was famous for some of the people who lived in the neighborhood, such as Mayor Thomas Bradley and Ray Charles. If you ever saw the movie "Ray", about the life of Ray Charles, a few of the scenes were shot in View Park. The thing I took back with me to Philadelphia was that LA had sunshine and blue skies!

Upon arriving back in Philadelphia on Tuesday, the first thing I noticed was that it was the same gray and dreary day when I left. But you know what? I didn't care! Why? Because I had seen the promise land and I was going to be living in it! This contrast made me even more excited about my future.

Deliverance

Several weeks before going to LA, Pastor Waters had been teaching during his Tuesday night bible study how God could deliver you from things. Things such as addictions, improper behavior, improper attitudes, etc. I have to admit, with less than two months before the wedding, I was still drinking. I had been drinking since 1970 or 25 years. Perhaps it was denial, but I didn't give drinking a lot of thought regarding my marriage. Well, that was all about to change.

I don't remember why I went to this club the Friday night after I had returned from LA. The club was on Delaware Ave in Philadelphia. I do remember that Bertha had sent me something intimate in the mail that I received a few days before, and I had it with me. So, I was in a great mood. Well, I got drunk, and I didn't know how to get to the subway, to get the R7 train, to get back to Chestnut Hill. Since moving to Chestnut Hill in September 1994, I hadn't ventured out, so I didn't know how the transportation system ran. The only thing I could think to do was to call my son George, Jr., who lived in West Philadelphia. I didn't want to call him, but I had no other choice.

George, Jr. came to pick me up and I was so ashamed. I could tell he was very embarrassed and upset with me. Well, I finally got home, but the next morning I felt more ashamed. I'm not sure if I even got out of bed. I do remember not going to Creative Word of Faith that Sunday. I also remember I didn't let Bertha know what happened that Friday night. I'm sure I spoke with her that Saturday and Sunday, letting on everything was fine. There is one thing I still remember. By Sunday, I had a strong, intense desire, to get to the Tuesday night bible study.

Pastor Waters was still teaching how God could deliver you. After bible study, I asked Pastor Waters if I could talk with him in his basement office. I explained to him what happened last Friday night. And then I said to him, "you said God can deliver. I want to be delivered from alcohol tonight!" We locked hands and he prayed and I agreed with him for about 20 minutes. When we were done, I didn't feel any different. I thanked him and Elder Wing gave me a ride home. After I got home, I called Bertha and told her everything, and she agreed with me for my deliverance.

Bertha's Anxiety

Focusing on time left was not one of my strengths, so I remember George saying 77 days. I zoned out from there on. I was just living one day at a time and taking care of Pennie and working in micro-lending. I attended community functions and interviewed businesses. There were many network functions, so I worked my business, FRAZIER FINANCIAL. I was an independent contractor. Homeowner loans were a part of my business. I was also appointed the chairperson of the Mayor's Economic Development Committee. I had no expenses so I had excess capital. Our honeymoon to Hawaii was paid for. All I needed was George and for time to pass.

When I got back to L.A. and began to look at the calendar I counted up the days in relation to my menses. May 20th would put me right into my cycle. I called George and asked him if that was okay. He answered, "stop the press". We would have to get another day. So we decided May 6, 1995, which was on a Saturday and the weather should be nice. Suzonne, from Crenshaw Christian Center Church, was the wedding coordinator assigned to help with the wedding particulars. I met with her and selected invitations. Our lists were gathered from George's side and mine. Boy, we needed to cut this down. My big family had lots of children. So rather than put that in the invitation, it was better for me to just tell everyone who might be bringing children. Many people from George's job asked to be invited. So I set aside rooms in a hotel in Marina del Rey for them. The invitations had an insert that read, "The bride and groom have established homes before. If you would like to bless them, may it be monetary or gift certificates so they might purchase what is needed or desired."

A restaurant called "Josephs" was to be used for the reception. I had met Joseph at a business function, and liked the way he worked. The limousine company was contacted, and we would have a brand new white stretch. Suzonne would make the decorations beautiful, and since we were having a "garden wedding", there was also a fountain in the background I used to sit at when I attended Pepperdine University, and where I took Felicia during that time for recess while I attended classes. The ambiance would be just beautiful. I took care and paid for all the expenses and made the proper deposits.

There was one glitch that needed immediate attention. My marriage to Billy had not been annulled. I was working on it. George did not know this. I had waited because once it was done, I would not have medical coverage. So here I am at the last minute, even though everything else is done, this behemoth had resurfaced. Had we married in Philadelphia, we would have to re-marry after this annulment to make our marriage legal. So I sought legal advice and ended up talking with Joanne's friend Mablean down at Superior Court, where I was trying to do it myself. She took the papers I had where Billy had filed for divorce, and looked at the proof I had where he had been married to his first wife, and crossed out divorce, circled annulment and told me to go downstairs and pay the clerk $185.00. She said don't set a wedding date (she did not know it was already done).

My next step, since the hearing would put me in jeopardy of being too close to May 6, was to convince Billy to agree to an earlier hearing date. This was daunting. He had been believing by his faith that he and I would re-marry. He enlisted some of his Christian brothers to stand in agreement with him. Well, I called him and told him I wanted to get our marriage off the books. He wanted to know what the rush was. He said, you are not planning to get married so leave things like they are. I insisted I needed him to sign the court document. So, finally he agreed to come over to 3719 Mt. Vernon Dr.

When he came over, he had so much news he wanted to catch me up on that I was trying to listen, but I had to focus on the signature. He would begin to sign, then talk about something else. He wanted me to pray for his health because he now had asthma. I did that. He wanted me to sit in his new car and look at all the bells and whistles. I did that. At last, in the midst of George's calling me to see what was taking so long, Billy signed. I wished him well and closed the door. I called George to let him know that it was done.

Billy promised to come to court, but he did not. The lawyer had told me he could be looking at penalties. Bigamy was a crime. When I went before the judge, I did not ask for any remuneration. George had already told me not to ask for part of anything, including Billy's pension. I only wanted my previous married name back. That, I was granted. When everything was completed and filed in the court, it was April 27, 1995! Whew, too close for comfort.

Sometime during the stress of the annulment and then the wedding proceedings Suzonne, noticed that I did not seem to be as animated as I should. So she asked me why I was not relaxing. She said everything was in place. I could not tell her everything, but I began to have break-through bleeding, and I went to the doctor. His remedy is he could do a procedure less invasive than a hysterectomy. My answer was no thank you. I did go to Church, and at this bible study, Minister Argie Taylor called for those needing healing. I responded to the invitation. When she laid her hands on me, she was silent for a while. Then she spoke under the anointing. "The Lord is restoring your body completely". I received that Word Of Knowledge and Word Of Wisdom. I have enjoyed divine health ever since. God Is Faithful. What I also didn't know was that Suzonne had called George, strongly suggesting that he come to L.A. to ease the anxiety I was facing.

In mid-March, George came to L.A. for his interview with Pastor Jimmy Price. George used the cassette tape of the wedding music I bought in Hawaii, along with other songs he selected for use for the wedding ceremony. I tried to show him as much of L.A. as I could. We went to the beach and he was thirsty and stated he wanted a beer? I said do you see people with beer or water. Everybody here is health conscious, so when you are thirsty, get some water. He met Joanne and Charles, my sister and brother-in-law. It was a rain storm, and the heel of his shoe came off in a puddle of water just before we went into their house. We found it and tacked it back on in the dark. It was a quick trip. During our interview with Pastor Jimmy, we kept hugging and holding hands. Pastor Jimmie kept laughing. He said, "George you got to be ready for this one....", meaning me. He was here for 4 days and went back to Philadelphia.

Pennie was my responsibility totally. So sometime down the line we made a decision that George would live with me and Pennie. So we would not be in Philadelphia after all. Enamored with the beauty of LA. George was hooked on sunshine and blue skies, mountains and beaches. Our banker friends were now fully aware that we were to be husband and wife, so they were all excited about George's coming to LA and joining the LAUB, the banker organization he had been president of in the Philadelphia Chapter.

George did finally come! It was April 29th. I was excited and Pennie was excited. I had to keep her focused on George, so that she would not be disengaged due to her Alzheimer's condition. I cleaned the house and Pennie helped. I was going to make tacos for dinner. He would not arrive until late, so I had Pennie hyped up such that she waited for us when I went to pick up George from the airport. Pulling into the driveway, we could see her looking out of the window. She wore one of her prettiest and most elegant hostess robes.

Despite all, she was a gracious lady.

We ate dinner, then went into my bedroom. Pennie came too. We sat and talked and looked at television. I said to George if she wants to sleep with us, that's fine. Pennie did get sleepy and went to her bedroom. When we awoke in the morning, I refreshed Pennie's memory. Her brother had the name George, so she was showing signs of endearment toward our new permanent houseguest. All was well.

Our wedding rehearsal was the next thing to take place. From the rehearsal, George would take his bags and go stay with his best man Jack until the wedding day. We woke up that morning, to find Pennie had left in the middle of the night. How frightening! We looked high and low, called the police and her cousins. How could this be happening? Where could she be? How did she get out? Well, about 2:30 in the afternoon, the Sherriff's Department brought Pennie home. She had been at least 7 miles from home in her nightgown. She knew her address, so here she is back home and in need of a bath. I bathed her and was re-thinking our plans to leave her while we were on our honeymoon, with people just checking in on her. Nobody wanted the responsibility. Her cousin took the initiative to locate a home for Pennie. No longer would she be riding in the limo with us or standing in place as mother for me. The new clothes I bought for her to wear at the wedding would not be used. Let me look for the blessing in this. Thank God for her safety.

CHAPTER 7
GET READY, GET READY, GET READY

George - Get Ready, Get Ready, Get Ready

The countdown was now underway for my exodus from Philadelphia on April 29, 1995. I was going to have a new wife, new house, new job, new geographical location with sunshine and blue skies most of the time, new church, a whole new life. Wow! When I seriously considered all of this, I remembered that audible voice from the Holy Spirit I heard back in January 1994 saying, "You need to be someplace else." Well, that statement was coming true! Praise God from whom all blessings flow!

On Saturday, April 16th , FE gave me a going away party. Many of my friends from CoreStates and the Philadelphia Chapter of the Urban Bankers Association came to our townhome. I struck up a conversation with a friend, whose named I believe was Ken, who I hadn't seen in a while, and he agreed to buy my furniture. He also agreed to give me a ride to Suburban Station in Center City Philadelphia so I could get the Airport Shuttle train to catch my flight. A friend of FE's worked for one of the airlines and as a wedding present, he let me fly free to LA, but I would be on standby.

A few days later, in the midst of packing, I ran across some things that I thought H would want. So I called her and she agreed to come to the townhome and get them. I don't remember when, but sometime between January 1995 and April 1995, I told H the whole story regarding Bertha and me. I knew she was hurt, but she knew the truth. Standing in the kitchen, I embraced her for the last time and I remember walking her to the door and watching her walk away. I truly hoped she would find a husband who would love her, respect her, and provide for her.

On Friday, April 29th the townhome was completely empty, except for a pillow and blanket that I slept with the night before. Ken picked me up and I'm off. I checked my bags and got to the boarding gate, letting them know that I had a standby ticket. Unfortunately, it was a full flight and I couldn't make that flight. After awhile, I'm beginning to get concerned, so I got the unction to go downstairs to the ticket counter. I told the airline representative my story (going to LA to get married) and I needed to get on the next flight. I don't know what she did, but I got a ticket for the next LA flight out and that was that.

One of the things I will always remember is rolling down the runway, leaving Philadelphia, and when the wheels left the ground, I felt as if I left all my past back in Philadelphia. I'm going some place else! By the way, I hadn't had a drink and hadn't thought about drinking since Pastor Waters and I prayed and agreed as men that I would be delivered from alcohol.

The Longest Flight

The flight from Philadelphia would take me to St Louis, where I had short time to wait for my connecting flight to LA. I called Bertha and let her know where I was and what time to expect me at LAX. Being on the flight to LA and leaving the ground was almost too exciting! I had a seat in the last row of the plane. My seat happened to be in the aisle, which I was thankful for. It was very difficult to keep still. Being in the isle, I was able to stretch my legs out completely, but I found myself sitting on the edge of my seat. I kept looking at my watch and was mindful of every minute. I was nervous. I wanted to feel the flight descending into LAX. I made idle conversation with passengers, but time seemed like it was going so slow. Finally, I felt the plane descending, and my heart was racing.

Bertha met me and we hugged and kissed in the terminal. Upon arriving at 3719 Mt Vernon, I noticed the time. It was close to 9PM LA time and that meant I had been traveling for close to 12 hours, from the time I left the townhome in the Chestnut Hill section of Philadelphia. I lived in the townhome for 8 months. As it turned out, Chestnut Hill was on the way to some place else.

Settling In – Sort Of

All during the month April, I had been mailing boxes of stuff to 3719 Mt Vernon Dr. On Saturday morning I began to unpack and put clothes and other belongings in my new closets and drawers. Pennie seemed really happy to see me and there was nothing but smiles and laughter at 3719 Mt Vernon Dr.

Bertha and I talked about the upcoming week. We were going to Crenshaw Christian Center Church on Sunday and on Monday we would begin to pack for our honeymoon to Hawaii on Sunday, May 7th. On Tuesday, we'd have our wedding rehearsal on the church grounds and then I was going to stay with Jack, who was going to be my best man, and his wife Faye.

In the early hours of Tuesday morning, I was awakened by what I thought was a door being shut. I paid it no mind and went back to sleep. I got up Tuesday morning and the house seemed unusually quiet. I don't remember whether I or Bertha mentioned it first, but Pennie was not in the house. We went outside in the back yard, but she wasn't there. We went out to the front yard and she wasn't there. We got in the car and drove around looking for Pennie, to no avail. We can back to the house and call the Sheriff's Department and they came to the house. We also called Penny's relatives, who were legally responsible for her and managed her finances and they came to the house. Pennie was 83 years old and Alzheimer's was beginning to set in. After a while, Pennie's relative left, and Bertha was very upset. Around 2PM, there was a knock on the door. We open the door and there's Pennie with 2 Sheriffs' Deputies. They found Pennie wondering around many blocks away near a major city street. She was still in her night gown and she didn't remember anything. After a while, Pennie's relatives came back and took Pennie with them. That was the last time Pennie would see 3719 Mt Vernon Dr.

With Pennie being OK, Bertha & I could focus on the

wedding rehearsal. I packed a suit case of clothes and stuff for my stay at Jack and Faye's, as well as my wedding day attire. The rehearsal lasted about 2 hours and it was time to say good-bye to my bride-to-be. We agreed to call each other over the three days.

Jack and Faye were both working so I had their house to myself. I would have three days of solitude. I remember I was reading Tom Clancy's new book called Debt of Honor. As I look back on it, my days were very peaceful and I had no anxiety. I often reflected on the moment. Here I am, getting ready to be married in a few days; to a woman I met 11 months ago. Wow! A brand new life!

Bertha's Bridal Shower

The rehearsal took place on Tuesday. George was disappointed because he felt I should be rehearsing as his wife-to-be. He did not want to hold to the tradition of a "stand in" person, who happened to be my friend Carolyn. Suzonne was in charge and this is what she said we would do. After the rehearsal, as planned, George took his bags and was off to stay with Jack and Faye in their beautiful Whittier, California home. I went home alone. Pennie was gone and George was at Jack's.

I adjusted to the solitude and continued to go over last minute details. Everything was in place. I packed two sets of clothes. One set to go with me for the church, and the other for the Honeymoon, including the white negligee George had seen in his vision of our wedding night. Saturday could not get here quick enough. I talked with George on the phone, not too long because I did not want to run up phone bills. He was reading a Tom Clancy book.

Two nights before the wedding, I received a phone call from a dear friend Janice, who asked who was giving me a bridal shower. I responded, "no one". She said, "you've got to be kidding? Your sisters are not giving you anything"? I said no. She asked me to give her a few names of some of my friends and their phone numbers. You would not believe what she did. She threw the biggest bridal shower you could imagine. She bought and decorated bottles of Snapple with "You Go Girl" on the bottles. She had a beautiful cake, vegetable trays, cheese trays, salad, and chicken and yes, we played games. What a friend! And the entire event was videotaped by Carolyn. There were gifts for the winners of the games.

Carolyn brought a song along for the bridal shower group to see to me. The melody is from the song by Stevie Wonder, "I Just Called to Say I Love You".

Deluge of Love

"Just For You Bertha"

We just want to say we love you Bertha
We just want to show how much we care
We just want to say we love you Bertha
And we mean it from the bottom of our hearts

We just want to say we love you Bertha
We just want to show how much we care
We just want to say we love you Bertha
And we mean it from the bottom of our hearts

Of our hearts ...Of our hearts

Bertha we're here ...to celebrate...
To share your joy and all those special things its brings
Your wedding's near...and we'll be there
To hear you say those little words like
"Yes, I Do"

This is why we're here to bless you
This deluge of love is just for you
So rejoice and let's be happy
Celebrating this time of joy with you

We just want to say we love you Bertha
We just want to show how much we care
We just want to say we love you Bertha
And we mean it from the bottom of our hearts
Of our hearts...Of our hearts

Carolyn had been told by Janice to make sure everybody went home early so that I could get some sleep. My sisters did not want to go home early. They stayed around until 12:00 midnight. They had to be ushered to the door. We had so much fun. Carolyn cleaned up the house and I did go to bed.

Wedding Day - May 6, 1995

Bertha – My Wedding Day

My Wedding Day was the most awesome day in my life! Everything went perfectly. The weather forecast had been rain. It had been raining several days. Plus it was windy and cold. However, George and I prayed the rain away, so it was a beautiful day! It was the only day in the week that was clear, with sunshine and blue skies.

My friend Sandy came over and got me, along with all my clothes. I had fun with the attendants who were assigned to help the bride. They did everything. My dress fit fine. My shoes were slipping on my feet, so Suzonne put double sided tape in them. Suzonne had a make-up bag for me and everything I could possibly need was there. We were early, as dictated by the Church. George sent a floral arrangement to me which was so sweet. Monica from the Spanish Ministry was there. She brought a card from the group.

Some of the wedding guests got there late. When the wedding started there was hardly anyone there. However, when we were presented as husband and wife, for the first time ever, there were many people in attendance.

George was handsome in his tuxedo. All the family and guests were trying to see what he looked like. No one had ever seen him. We talked to each other throughout the ceremony when there was only music playing because we had missed each other those few days. The photographer took many photos at the wedding. Sam (my brother-in-law) and Derek (Sam's son) videotaped the entire wedding and reception, and my sister Joyce and Sam later gave the video to us as a wedding gift. It was the best gift we received, and it keeps on giving each year around our anniversary time when we view it. The photographer did not show up at the reception.

As a mature bride, I looked better than I did when I was 20. We danced and had the fun we expected. The money dance proved lucrative. The Electric Slide to Alicia Bridges, "I Love the Nightlife", was perfect!

The Reception was full of people, so much so that I had to pay another $1500.00 for all the food they ate! There were people at the reception I never saw at the wedding. When we left in the limo to travel a short distance to our hotel in Marina Del Rey, Jack and Faye came to take our wedding clothes home with them, so that we could just leave for our honeymoon in the morning with the clothes we needed for Hawaii.

I tried to shower and come out of the bathroom in my white negligee like George imagined. However, we were hungry. We ordered room service since we did not get to eat anything at the reception. We ate the top layer of our cake, which was supposed to be reserved for the first anniversary, consummated our marriage, and went to sleep. We really didn't discover each other's bodies until we got to Hawaii. We were so compatible. God knew what He was doing when he brought us together. He just required our obedience. Everything was so smooth. GOD IS FAITHFUL!

George – My Wedding Day

The Day had finally arrived! Since the wedding was at 1PM sharp, we left Jack & Faye's about 10AM. On the way to the church, Jack stopped at a Walgreen's store to pick up something. That something turned out to be smelling salts. Bertha had told Jack to pick it up in case I needed it! Her rationale was that when my first son was born, I fainted in the delivery room, so she wasn't taking any chances. The truth of the matter was I hyperventilated while helping my wife breath during delivery. As soon as my son was born, the nurse handed him to me, but I had the presence of mind to give the baby back to the nurse. As I walked out of the delivery room, Boom! I hit the floor. I didn't need the smelling salts for my wedding.

After getting dressed in our tuxedos, the photographer began taking pictures of Jack and me as well as Bertha's son Faaron, who would be giving his mother away in marriage. At 12:30PM, I walked out to the garden area where the wedding was going to take place. There was no one in the audience, which at the time didn't seem to phase me. I was where I was supposed to be and I was sure Bertha was where she was supposed to be. At approximately, 12:45PM, the first guests arrived. At that point, I was oblivious to the audience. My focus was on Jack and I getting in position to walk up the aisle. At exactly 1PM, with Pastor Jimmy in place, Jack and I started walking up the aisle to Love Said, Not So, by BeBe Winans.

Next followed Sandy, Bertha's Matron of Honor. Once Sandy was in place, about 30 second had passed before we began to hear Gladys Knight's song, You're the Best Thing That Ever Happened to Me, as Bertha began her entrance. Bertha was wearing the wedding dress and the veil she bought in the Chestnut Hill section of Philadelphia when she came to visit me in December. She looked wonderful in her dress and she was radiant! The wedding ceremony and vows were from Kenneth Copeland's Wedding Ceremony Book, and at a certain portion of the ceremony, the song, Here and Now, by Luther Vandross was played. The song was so appropriate to the way I felt towards Bertha and our marriage.

After the song ended, Pastor Jimmy informed us of our marriage blessings coming from the Wedding Ceremony Book, most notably from Deuteronomy 28:1-14. After that, Pastor Jimmy pronounced us husband and wife, followed by our kiss and embrace. It was time for us to be introduced for the first time as Mr. & Mrs. George Ronald Toulson, Sr. The time was exactly 1:30PM and there were very few empty seats in the audience.

After walking down the aisle, we and members of the family formed a greeting line. After that ended, the photographer wanted to take what amounted to the bulk of the wedding photos, although Felicia took just as many. But before that happened, Bertha and I stole away behind the wedding backdrop to a water fountain and I remember clearly looking her in the eyes and saying, "Honey, we did it". At that point, the Holy Spirit showed me in an instant, the 11 months that lead up to this point in time. I will always remember that moment.

The Reception

Our wedding reception was a lot of fun. After the toast from Jack, my best man, Betty and Yvonne (from the LA Chapter of Urban Bankers Association) toasted us by noting that they were responsible for our union, as well as Eleanor, Bertha's best friend, who said she had been praying for her Bertha to find a good husband. And, she admonished me that, "...you better be good to my friend". Felicia got in her toast by saying had her mother not come to DC, Bertha wouldn't have met me. You'll have to go back and read Bertha's account of her interaction with Felicia back in DC to get the meaning of Felicia's statement.

After the wedding bouquet and garter tossing, came the money dance, where anyone that wanted to dance with Bertha or me, had to give us money. While the dance was quite lucrative, some family members were accused of X putting some money in and taking more money out. I didn't believe it, but that's what was said.

CHAPTER 8
OUR HONEYMOON NIGHT

Go back and read, "The Vision" letter I wrote to Bertha. That letter sums up pretty much our honeymoon night.

Honolulu, HI

The trip to Hawaii on May 7, 1995 was our first time completely alone since January 1, 1995. I can still remember what it felt like being with my wife going on our honeymoon. We talked the whole 5 hour flight to Honolulu, HI. I had a window seat and I can still remember seeing the Hawaii Island chain, with its lush green landscape, mountains, and blue colored water.

We stayed at the Outrigger Hotel and on the beach we took

many pictures with Diamond Head as the backdrop. While on the beach, Bertha was in her bikini and I was in a speedo. The weather was beautiful in the mid 80's. We'd be at the Outrigger for 4 days and travel to Maui for another 3 days.

We decided to get information on the various excursions and decide on the Polynesian, the Arizona Memorial at Pearl Harbor tours, and an all day air-condition bus tour of the island of Oahu. We learned a little about the Polynesian cultural and history and took many, many pictures which we still view each year around our anniversary date.

Maui, HI

In Maui, we spent a lot of time in our hotel room. We had a balcony that overlooked the beautifully blue Pacific Ocean. Bertha took a picture of me sitting on the balcony as I was pondering our future. We went to an Hawaiian luau and danced the hula. One day, we woke up at 2AM and took a three hour bus ride to an inactive volcano over 10,000 feet up, which was above the clouds and watched the sun rise.

Without a doubt, our wedding and honeymoon was the best week we've ever had. Nothing, absolutely nothing, went anywhere near wrong during this time. I don't know how God could have blessed us more.

Upon arrival back at 3719 Mt Vernon Dr, we got a little carried away with some of the memories of our wedding and honeymoon. We got dressed up in some of our wedding and honeymoon attire, somewhat scandalously, and we took pictures of each other and used a wall with mirrors to enhance some of the photos of us together. These photos are under lock and key. We also review these photos around our anniversary date.

UBA Conference – 1995

In 1995, the Urban Bankers Association National Conference was held in Boston, MA. As I mentioned earlier, oftentimes conferences such as these lead to things that have nothing to do with banking related issues. One such thing was a philandering Philadelphian meeting a conservative Californian getting married as a result of the previous year's conference.

Well, Bertha and I were the hit of the conference. Many people would stop and chat with us and/or congratulate us. Members of the Philadelphia and Los Angeles chapters were especially gracious. On June 6, 1995, my best man Jack and several friends gave us a surprise newlywed party. There was a nice gathering of 25-30 people. They had cake with Congratulations George & Bertha written on it, fruit salad, and Champaign. I took a sip of Champaign and said to myself, "I can't do this", and that was the last time alcohol has touch my lips.

All in all, we had a wonderful time at the conference. I personally had done some serious travelling – from Philadelphia to LA to get married, from LA to Hawaii for our honeymoon and back, from LA to Boston and back to LA from the UBA conference, all in about a 40 day period of time.

First Year of Marriage

Our first year of marriage was very exciting, especially for me. Bertha had lived and worked in Southern California for many years. She started out with the Los Angeles County Department, which was the largest in population of any county in the US. She held various positions with the county, including using her Spanish speaking skills in many positions that she held. She later graduated Summa Cum Laude from Pepperdine University and started her banking career with First Interstate Bank.

For me, everything and every place was new. Of course, we went around and met family members and friends, but it took me quite a while to distinguish between the Los Angeles, Inglewood and Culver City city limits. We were situated such that a five minute drive east of us, put us in Inglewood, CA and a five minute drive south would put us in Culver City, CA. The best way to describe the Southern California freeways is that in the Philadelphia metropolitan area, you have one interstate highway, which is I-95, which runs from Maine to Florida. In Southern California, you have the 1, 5, 10, 57, 60, 91, 101, 105, 110, 210, 405, 605, and the 710. The term "road rage" originated in Southern California. These 13 routes, especially the 10, 60, 110, and 405 were always bumper to bumper, no matter what time of day or night.

It was pretty cool to visit all the places you've heard about, such as Hollywood, Beverly Hills, Rodeo Drive, the Hollywood sign, Venice Beach, and driving up the Pacific Coast Highway (Route 1). On a clear day, you could look north easterly and see the snow capped mountains from where we lived in View Park.

An unexpected turn of events with Pennie, left Bertha and I in a house all to ourselves. The only expense to the house was utilities and Bertha's car was paid for. This blessing lasted 4 ½ years.

Crenshaw Christian Center

Shortly after returning from Boston, I joined Crenshaw Christian Center (CCC) Church, whose founder and pastor was Dr. Frederick K. C. Price, and home of the Faith Dome, a 10,000+ seating facility, and the largest Dome church in the United States. The church was very structured in their praise and worship and main church service, as well as the Helps Ministry. The Helps Ministry was a collection of service organizations designed to facilitate any need a church member would require. The Sunday church service was taped and taught over Pastor Price's Ever Increasing Faith television program, and broadcast nationally and in many countries all over the world . The ushers, who were all men, and the musicians and choir members, were very good and disciplined. I marveled at the church structure, but I really enjoyed Pastor Price's teaching style and his focus on the teaching of Faith. Pastor Price was always impeccably dressed, as well as his wife Dr. Betty Price, and most of the church members dressed impeccably as well.

Coming off the teaching I received from Pastor Waters at Creative Word of Faith Church, Pastor Price's ministry was the natural progression for me in the teaching of Faith. Many pastors and evangelists have their message and pastoral styles, but I believe the only other pastor of note that taught about Faith exclusively was Kenneth Copeland. Pastor Price usually taught a series of teachings and the most famous of his teachings, "Race, Religion, & Racism", lasted for 76 weeks, beginning in 1997. I believe Bertha and I were there for each of the 76 weeks, except for the Christmas week of 1997, due to us being in Delaware. The series was ground breaking and controversial, and we enjoyed the whole series.

Once a man or a woman became a member of CCC, they were automatically members of the Men's or Women's Fellowship ministry, but if you wanted to join any other ministries of the church, you had to wait a year to be eligible to join.

There was Bible Study Monday through Saturday during the day and in the evening, administered by 10 pastors, including Dr. Price, whose Bible Study was Tuesday night at 7:30. When possible, I attended the Tuesday night Bible Study.

Alcohol Deliverance Confirmation

In August 1995, I went into a Ralph's Super Market store to cash a check. As I walked into the store, I saw the banking branch to my right and quite a long line of folks in the teller line. So, I made my way to the back of the line. What are the things people do standing in line? Today you can check your e-mail or send/answer text messages. At the time I could do neither. So, I'm just standing there. Then I get an unction from the Holy Spirit that said, "open your eyes". At that moment, I notice that I'm standing in the liquor isle of Ralph's. All around me was alcohol in all the various forms. That's when I knew that I was totally and completely delivered from alcohol. God had removed all experiences I had with alcohol, even the taste. I also had the unction that I was also delivered from the lusts of women. This was a glorious day in my life, a day I won't forget and I thanked God and informed Bertha. As of this writing, it's been approximately 14 ½ years since alcohol has touched my lips.

Christmas - 1995

Christmas 1995 would usher in a travel itinerary that took us back to Newark, Delaware, where I was born and raised for the next four Christmas'. Neither my Mom or Dad, or any of my grown children came to the wedding, so it was a time to be re-united with my east coast family. When we announced to the family that we were coming to Newark for Christmas, my daughter Angie got real busy and planned her wedding so I could walk her down the isle, which I did on December 30, 1995. Bertha and I also invited Pastor Charles & Mary Waters of Creative Word of Faith Church, where Pastor Waters prayed and agreed with me for my deliverance from alcohol, to visit with us at my Mom & Dad's. We had a wonderful time with family during our first Christmas as a married couple.

First Job

In July 1995, I took a job selling computer training at a company in Torrance, CA. This company was a very large provider of computer hardware and software. At that time, the aerospace industry in Southern California was experiencing difficulty and there were a lot of layoffs. Computing training, especially the Microsoft Certified Systems Engineer (MCSE) designation was in very high demand, and the US government would pay for the training. After about 6-8 month working at this company, the management at this company wanted to get in on this lucrative revenue generator. The company looked to the department head in charge of Computer Training, whose name was "V". "V" was the company's biggest sales representative of computer hardware and software, whose sole client was a very large mortgage company. "V" didn't care much for the Computer Training Department, but because of her high profile, she got stuck with it. She mentioned this chore to my boss and I began to think how the MCSE training would work. Since I was already selling computer training, I knew and worked with instructors who knew MCSE instructors. I put a plan together and gave it to my boss who passed it on to "V".

The plan called for hiring MCSE certified instructors, paying them a certain amount of money per class, determining an optimal class size, and acquiring the required course and software curriculum. I then put a cost to all of this and a sale price per student. I put a 40% mark-up over the cost, and had myself and another salesman "B", make a very nice commission percentage per student. I don't remember the price I established, but we earned a 20% commission, which "B" & I split 50/50 per student. We put all this in writing in the form of a commission agreement, and "V" said OK, without really questioning me about the numbers, which surprised me and "B". My financial analyst work experience served me well.

With this done, the company began to advertise that they had a school for MCSE training. The government required that a student would have to visit, and show documentation of each visit to three schools offering the training. So, "B" and I had to meet and greet prospective students and SELL them on the company's MCSE program. The selling was fun and exciting. The company had a great training facility, so that part was easy. We were competing against three other well known schools of computer training that already had an MCSE training program.

The number of students in our first class was far better than I had forecast, and every student enrolled received their MCSE certification. We had a graduating party for the students and

"B" and I were seeking referrals from the happy graduating, soon to be employed students. "B" and I had made a lot of money, so much so that it caught the attention of "V" and the company's management. How dare two salesman make so much money, but we had a commission agreement, so in that regard, there was nothing they could do to change the commission agreement. When we began gearing up for the 2nd class, "V" brought in a woman to "help" us with the program. "B" and I knew what was coming. Before "B" and I began to meet and greet and SELL the next set of students, I was fired for something that didn't make any sense, and everybody in the computer training department knew it. This was September 1996. In talking with a few of the other employees in the department after I left, I discovered that the second group of students were far fewer than expected, and not all of them graduated. After the second group of students, the company didn't offer the MACE class any longer, and the company dissolved the computer training department altogether.

Second Year of Marriage – 1996

On May 6, 1996, Bertha and I celebrated our one year wedding anniversary by having dinner at Joseph's, the restaurant where we had our wedding reception. We looked back on our wedding, reception and honeymoon, the one year that had transpired, and we were very happy and thankful to God. We knew that God is faithful!

Trouble In Paradise

After losing the job in September 1996, I immediately signed up and received 26 weeks of unemployment. It wasn't very much per week. With the success I had with MCSE training class at the company, I wanted to be in my own business, using my skills as a financial analyst, and the MCSE experience. Thus, I formed The Toulson Group. I bought a Dell Desktop computer and software, printer, and work station. I began to write a business plan for an Executive Training Program, consisting of a Dell Notebook and related software, Microsoft Office, Hewlett Packard printer and a training curriculum to train executives (really anyone who wanted such training) so that they would be more effective and efficient in their business or job. I contacted some of the company's ex-computer trainers, staff folks, and a couple of salesmen and I laid at my plan. I rented office space at the Kilroy Center near the Los Angeles International Airport (LAX) and I had a staff, with a receptionist, printing and faxing capabilities that came with the rental space. I had a totally professional environment. During 1995-1996, the Internet was the biggest thing since the personal computers in 1983, and I was going to capitalize on what was going on in the market, or so I hoped. However, I lacked two critical components, which I believe doomed my fate even before I really got started. Those two components were capital and a well thought out marketing plan. One of the computer trainers invested his own personal funds in the business because he believed in what I was doing and he knew me. But I couldn't get any other investors. I didn't know who they were or who I could contact that knew who they were. I moved into the Kilroy Center in October 1996, and moved out the end of December 1996.

Prior to our wedding, Bertha's contract with Community Financial Resource Center had expired and she wasn't working, although she had some money set aside. She really didn't like the job I had at the computer training company because it was a salary plus commission job. The base salary was $18,000. I actually didn't like the job either because the job mainly consisted of telephoning companies asking them to send their employees to the company for their computer training needs. So, after I got fired from the company, Bertha expected me to get a job. To be honest, I didn't want a job. I wanted to be in my own business. I've wanted to have my own business since I graduated from the University of Delaware in 1975. However, Bertha supported me when I explained the concept of the Executive Training program to her. She also helped me move out of the Kilroy Center in December 1996.

At this point, I had no job or business, but I was still sitting at home at the work station trying to make something happen. I was able to get a couple of temporary assignments that only lasted a week here and a week there. However, Bertha was beginning to get agitated seeing me sit at the work station day in and day out. I had never seen this side of her and I didn't like what I saw, but what could I say? We began to argue, something that we never did before. Voices got raised and yelling appeared. We decided to call Pastor Waters back in Philadelphia. I'm sure we talked about my role as a husband in providing for my wife, which was all about generating income. Generating income would be a re-occurring challenge to me through the ensuing years.

If there was a bright side to arguing and generating income challenges, it was that I began to pray in earnest about my marriage and generating income. I always felt more comfortable walking around while I was praying, as opposed to praying on my knees, so I began to walk around the dining room table as I prayed. I remember it like it was yesterday. I tried to pray what scriptures I knew, which weren't a lot at this time in my Christian walk. Sometimes I would pray the Word from the bible as I was walking.

One prayer that I developed at this time of my life that gave me peace and has always stuck with me is a prayer that I call the Holy Spirit Prayer. It reads as follows:

Holy Spirit Prayer

Father, I thank you for your Word, for your Word is truth and your Word is life, and it will not return unto you void, but will accomplish your divine decree. (Isaiah 55:11)

Father, I thank you that your Word declares that greater is He that lives in me then he that is in the world. (1 John 4:4)

Holy Spirit, I thank you for teaching me the things of God and bringing all things to my remembrance. (John 14:26)

Holy Spirit, I thank you for dwelling in me and for comforting me (John 14: 7, John 14:26). I thank you for guiding me in all that I say and in all that I do. Because Holy Spirit I know, that by standing on God's Word and with your guidance, I will rise above all situations and all circumstances (my financial situation, my credit situation, and my tax situation) and I will be victorious in all that I set my hands to.

The Newlywed Game

What I didn't know then, back in 1996, is that even in the midst of trials or challenges, God can still bless you in ways you could never imagine. Bertha & I were about to get blessed.

Janice, the dear friend of Bertha who was responsible for organizing her bridal shower gave Bertha a flyer (I still have it) that read as follows:

Recently Married?

Engaged?

THE NEWLYWED
GAME
WANTS YOU!!!

If you've been married
2 years or less
OR
If you're engaged to be
married within the next
6 months

Call

213-860-8484

Bertha called the number! We then were invited to Hollywood, CA to interview for a new version of The Newlywed Game show. On the day we were at the studio, there had to be 20-25 couples interviewing. I have no idea how many couples were interviewed in total.

In a letter dated June 26, 1996, from the contestant producer, it read:

Dear Contestant Applicant,

CONGRATULATIONS! You have been placed in our "Newlywed Game" active contestant file. When we interviewed you we were not aware that we needed to see your original marriage certificate. We need to see the certificate that was signed by the person who married you (NOT your marriage license, which is easy to falsify). If you are having trouble locating the certificate, the County Recorder's office has it on file.

There's more to the letter, but this was the most important part. We were going to be on The Newlywed Game show!

On the day of our taping of the show, we spent a few hours with the other three couples. This provided comradery among the husbands and wives, for the show wanted to display husbands getting along with each other as well as the wives getting along with each other. We also spent time with the production staff so they could find out interesting tidbits about each couple that they could use during the taping.

The production staff didn't tell us (the contestants) that they planned to use as a theme for this particular Newlywed Game show, "Married Couples – The Second Time Around", in that all of the contestants had been married before. This of course would provide all sorts of questions comparing our current marriage to the previous marriage.

When the show went live, we were the first couple introduced, and the show host (Gary Kroeger, not Bob Eubanks) took a few seconds to comment about us. He mentioned the fact that Bertha put together a list of 53 things she wanted in a husband, and she checked it twice, to which Bertha said, "and George measured up to all of them". Gary did this with each couple.

At the end of the first round of questions, Bertha and I were tied for the lead with couple #2. At the end of the second round, we were tied with couple #4. During the 2nd round, yours truly, gave the reason for his answer to a question and he got up and high fived the other three husbands. During the same round, another husband gave his reason for his answer, and he proceeded to high five the other three husband, to which the wives shook their heads and the live audience loved it.

At the end of the third and final round, we were still tied for the lead with another couple. Fifteen points separated the leaders from last place. We were informed that the winner would receive an all expenses paid trip to Dutch St. Maarten, in the Netherlands Antilles, directly north of Barbados, and stay 7 days and 6 nights at the Horney Toad Guesthouse, a former governor's house. The bonus question was worth 25 points, so it was still anyone's game.

The couple in last place was the first to be asked the bonus question, which they answered correctly, and moved into first place. The third place couple missed the question, and they dropped to last place. The couple that we were tied with also missed the bonus question. So, Bertha and I were in second place and if I answered the question correctly, we'd be going to Dutch St. Maarten. But before I could answer, Gary made me wait and tried to make me squirm. I had my answer. I hoped Bertha chose the same answer. In case you're wondering, the question was this. "In approaching the time of "making whoopee", do I perform a sneak attack or does Bertha see it coming". I answered without hesitation, "she sees it coming" (the correct answer). I leaped straight up like I was going for a rebound and began dancing around the stage. I had forgotten about Bertha and was reminded she was going too. So I ran over to her, picked her up and swung her around. I had never won anything in my life and we're going to Dutch St. Maarten for 7 days and 6 nights, all expenses paid! Was this a blessing or what???

Our Show Airs

We taped the show in October and we were later told it would air in November. The show aired on a Tuesday at 10:30AM. We told a few of our west coast friends and family. We were excited!

The show came on and there was George & Bertha Toulson. There was interaction between the couples and everybody seemed excited. We got through the first round of questions, with the Toulson's tied for first place. Then came a commercial break. As soon as the break started, across the TV screen flashed, "BREAKING NEWS STORY'. There was a police chase on one the highways in Los Angeles County. Some fool had robbed a bank and the airing of our Newlywed Game show was pre-empted to follow the chase. I screamed in anger and called Satan a liar! I couldn't believe this was happening to us. If Jesus was coming back, and the news media had their way, they'd pre-empt Jesus to show a car chase on a California freeway! The show was only 30 minute and the pre-emption lasted for 40 minutes. Unbelievable!

What a disappointment! After allowing myself to calm down, I remembered the producer said we'd get a copy (VCR tape) of the show. Around 11:30AM the phone rang, and it was some of our Las Vegas friends who saw the show. They got a kick at of my antics. Later that evening, we get another call. This time its from my youngest son who's a pre-med student at the University of North Carolina. He said he was flipping through channels and there was Dad and Bertha on the Newlywed Game show. He said he was able to watch almost all the show.

We did receive a VCR copy of the show, and we usually watch it at least once a year. I watched it again, especially for this writing.

St. Maarten

Our trip was scheduled the first week in February 1997. We flew from Los Angeles to Miami, then to Dutch St. Maarten. It always was exciting to travel with Bertha and it seemed like we were always going someplace new. I had a window seat and it seemed like the runway was on the beach, and the beach goers seemed way too close.

According to Wikipedia, on March 23, 1648, France and the Dutch Republic agreed to divide the island between their two nations, so they signed the Treaty of Concordia. The island is served by many major airlines that bring in large jet aircrafts, including Boeing 747's, Airbus A340's, and McDonnell Douglas MD-11's carrying tourists from across the world on a daily basis. The short length of the main runway at Princess Juliana International Airport, and its position between a large hill and a beach causes some spectacular approaches. Aviation photographers flock to the airport to capture pictures of large jets just a few meters above sunbathers on Maho Beach.

The Horny Toad Guesthouse was composed of 8 fully equipped apartments. One of the things I remembered at night in our apartment was the sound of the waves pounding the beach, which was rather steep for a beach. Every evening at 5:30, most of the guests in Horny Toad would meet at the beach and have drinks and hors d'oeuvre. We'd talk about what we each did that day and took note of maybe where to go the next day.

According to Wikipedia, St. Martin's Dutch side is known for its festive nightlife, beaches, jewelry, exotic drinks made with native rum-based guavaberry liquors, and plentiful casinos, while its French side, is known more for its nude beaches, clothes, shopping (including outdoor markets), and rich French and Indian Caribbean cuisine. The island is home to accommodations including hotels, villas, and timeshares, many of which are privately available for rent or sale.

Keep in mind that in February 1997, revenue coming in was slim to none. We had just started our SBA Loan Intermediary business, which I'll talk about later, and we only had a few hundred dollars that came in so far. However, the favor of God is worth far more than money. One of the couples staying at the guesthouse took us around in their rental car and we saw much of the island, including the French side. They also paid for our lunch on a couple of occasions. During the time we were there, the film "Speed 2" was being shot on the French side of the island. The film set had a cutaway of an actual bow section of a cruise ship, depicting the cruise ship running aground. We watched a little bit of the filming and went on our way.

As a result of our success on the Newlywed Game the producer used us as contestants for several pilot games shows that didn't get on the air. We also did Aerobed infomercials which aired on late night cable channels. The game show pilots and infomercials lasted for several months.

Needless to say, Bertha and I had a wonderful time as a result of the Newlywed Game exposure. We knew we were being blessed because God is faithful.

CHAPTER 9
1997

Year 1997

In the last quarter of 1996, Bertha got involved with the Minority Business Opportunity Committee (MBOC) of the Mayor's Office in Los Angeles. Richard J. Riordan was the mayor. In particular, Bertha got involved with the Finance Committee component of MBOC, based on her experience being a branch manager for First Interstate Bank and working with the Community Financial Resource Center (CFRC) making loans to businesses hard hit by the January 1994 earthquake. Bertha had extensive experience going out into the various communities: African–American, Hispanic and the Asian communities. While on the Finance Committee, which she would later chair, she met the 2nd in command of the Los Angeles District of the Small Business Administration (LASBA). At the time, the LASBA was the largest and most creative of all the SBA districts in the USA, and Bertha and I we were about to be blessed. This gentleman was looking for a business that could work with the LASBA in helping small businesses obtain capital through the SBA's Loan Intermediary Program. The program worked like this. A small business would call into the LASBA office and depending on where their business would be operating from, via zip code, would determine which SBA Loan Intermediary would work with them. The Toulson Group (TTG) became an SBA Loan Intermediary and our territory was from Santa Monica to down to the Los Angeles International Airport (LAX). I don't recall the exact zip codes. What we would do as an SBA Loan Intermediary was to meet with clients, analyze their business plan, critique it, re-write it, or write a business plan for their business from scratch. We charged $3,000 to create a business plan and $1,800 to modify an existing business plan. We had only one client whose business plan was prefect (a telecommunications company). The client also needed a minimum credit score of 620, where TTG would pull their credit report and include it as part of the documentation. The client needed to have real estate for collateral, as this was the SBA's preferred form of collateral. Given a reasonable business plan, which the SBA would examine in detail, they would guarantee 80% of the loan. TTG would present this "loan package" to banks that funded SBA loans. The banks in turn would give us a 3% finders fee for bring them the loan.

Over the course of 15 months (Oct 1996 – Dec 1997), we put together 9 loan packages, of which 6 got funded. The largest loan package was for $250K and the smallest was $50K. In January 1998, the SBA started using non-profit SBA Loan Intermediaries and with TTG being a for-profit business, that revenue source ended.

Year 1998

In January 1998, while working with a temporary employment agency, I landed a position as a consultant to the Los Angeles Times, Southern California's leading newspaper. This assignment would be for one year and pay $40K. My financial and systems analyst background helped me secure this position. My primary duty was to design and analyze online scripts used for a whole host of purposes. I worked in downtown Los Angeles and got a chance to tour downtown.

On May 6, 1998, Bertha and I celebrated our 3rd year wedding anniversary by driving to San Diego and spent a few days sightseeing. We had dinner at the Hotel Del Coronado.

Bertha was ending her time as Finance Committee Chair of the Minority Business Opportunity Committee (MBOC). She had been a refreshing voice and dedicated leader of the committee for a year. On May 20, 1998, Bertha was presented a 2.5 ft by 2.5 ft framed citation and photos of her and Mayor Richard J. Riordan, along with photos with other members of MBOC. The citation read as follows:

The Toulson Group

In recognition of your outstanding leadership and commitment to the Los Angeles Minority Business Opportunity Committee and embracing the principals of partnership and participation. Your efforts as Chair of the Finance Sub-Committee have helped to provide the minority, women, and disadvantage business enterprise community with better access to capital providers.

Richard J. Riordan

The year 1998 was the best year financially that we had since 1995. Again, we thanked God for in faithfulness.

Year 1999

The Year 1999 would prove to be a life changing year for Bertha and me. A few months after the LA Times Consulting assignment ended in January 1999, the challenge of generating revenue was again upon me. Bertha wasn't working and I began to feel inadequate, in not being able to provide for my wife. I began to pray every morning for God to do something to help me generate revenue, whether through a job or a business opportunity. I contacted many of the temp agencies in LA, but I wasn't getting any assignments. I looked in the LA Times Employment Section. Bertha felt I wasn't looking hard enough for a job and she was beginning to make her feelings known loud and clear.

Bertha swallowed her pride and took a job as a teller at Union Bank. She was a former Bank Branch manager, but in order to support us she was taking this job, working 35 hours a week. It was demeaning for her, but she strived to be the best teller she could be. To make matters worse, the Branch Manager at the bank knew Bertha from her involvement with the LA chapter of the Urban Bankers. I felt ashamed. There were many days I walked around the house clutching my bible to my chest, with tears coming down my face, praying to God for a job. These were extremely tense times. I read scriptures, I prayed, I cried. Bertha didn't know this. It would be a few years before I told her what I was doing.

On Monday, October 25, 1999, I got a call from my youngest son Charles. He was at my Mom and Dad's house and he was crying. He was crying because Dad had just been diagnosed with cancer that had spread so rapidly (we didn't know he had cancer) that the doctors said he probably had less than a week to live. Bertha and I had to get back to Newark, DE immediately, but I didn't have the airfare. How hurtful and embarrassing this was. I told my son Charles and he wired $700 for Bertha and me to fly to Philadelphia.

We got a flight out early Friday morning and we arrived at the Philadelphia International Airport around 6PM. My son George, Jr. picked us up from the airport. He was visibly tired because he lived in West Philadelphia, and every day since Monday, he would travel to Newark to pick up Mom and take her to the hospital to see Dad. You see, I was an only child, and while I lived in LA for 4 ½ years, George, Jr. was the one who looked in on Mom and Dad on a regular basis.

When Bertha and I got to the hospital, Dad was awake. He smiled at us and he seemed in good spirits. Mom was there, and I believe Demetria my oldest daughter and Rosalind, my ex-wife were also there. Hospice care for Dad had already been set up and the hospice person was there as well, letting us know that Dad would be coming home mid-Saturday afternoon.

Back at Mom and Dad's house, the house I grew up in as a child, everything was in place for Dad to come home. Angie, my second daughter was also there and she had her second child with her, Jasmine, who was just born on September 27th. At about 3PM we called the hospital who said the ambulance had just left. Normally on a Saturday at that time of the day, the trip from the hospital to our house would take about 20-25 minutes. 4PM came and Dad wasn't home yet. We called the hospital wondering what was taking so long and we were informed that the driver was lost. Well, you can imagine what we as a family were feeling. Finally, at about 5:30, the ambulance pulls in to the driveway. The driver apologized and I accepted his apology.

Dad was placed in the bed that was put up in the living room. Bertha, Mom, Charles, Angie and I went to Dad's bedside and took his hand, smiled, and we all said how happy we were that he was home. I took baby Jasmine and showed her to Dad. Dad smiled and said, "hey baby". I left the bedside, put Jasmine down, and came back to stand with Mom and Charles. We notice that Dad seemed like he was looking at something. He even gestured with his right hand. Mom was talking to him, and I turned away and began taking with the hospice person. After about a minute, I heard Mom say, "Charlie, open your eyes and talk to us." I turned around to see Dad, but Dad was gone. The last words Dad said were "hey baby" as he spoke to baby Jasmine. I looked at my watch and it was exactly 6PM. He lived about 30 minutes after arriving home.

We had Dad's funeral the following Saturday and it was a wonderful "home going celebration". A few days after the funeral, I woke up in the bedroom I grew up in as a child, and it occurred to me that I was not going back to Los Angeles. Who was going to take care of Mom? I couldn't ask my son George, who lived at least an hour away to take care of her. She was now my responsibility. Bertha and I talked about this and she agreed with me. We'd be leaving Los Angeles and moving to Newark, DE. All the while living in Los Angeles, it never occurred to me that I'd ever move back to Newark, DE. I began to think about what I heard in an audible voice in January 1994 – "You need to be some place else". What did that truly mean?

Time of Reflection

I believe 1995-1999 was a period of faith building in my spirit, soul, and body. My seed of faith really began to grow in me on May 6, 1995 when I spoke my wedding vows and Bertha and I were pronounced husband and wife. In April 1997, I met with Pastor Jimmy Price and I gave him what I thought were my goals at the time. What he gave me were 7 sets of different scriptures that have been the foundation of my life going forward from April 1997, and by way of extension, Bertha's life too. These scriptures were as follows:

1 Kings 17:1-9   King James Bible (God sustains us)
Psalm 91: 1-16   Amplified Bible (God allows us to abide under his shadow)
1 Cor 10:13   Amplified Bible (God is faithful)
Phil 4: 19   King James Bible (God supplies all our need)
Deut 28: 1-14   King James Bible (God's blessings & promises to us)
Isa 54:17   King James Bible (No weapon formed against us shall prosper)
2 Tim 1:7   King James Bible (God has not given us the spirit of fear)

Through the Years

From 2000-2010 these scriptures will have a significant impact on our lives, as well as the lives of our family and others. For in 2000, we joined Victory Christian Fellowship Church in New Castle, DE and the first of many shoots brought on by my seed of faith that began to grow in 1995, broke through good ground.

CHAPTER 10
2000

Year 2000

Bertha and I decided that after Thanksgiving 1999, she'd fly back to Los Angeles. Once there she would begin packing and sending boxes to Newark. We had talked to a good friend in LA about our situation in Delaware and he asked what we were going to do with 3719 Mt. Vernon Dr? We hadn't thought about it. So he asked if he could stay there for 30 days and he would pay us rent. We said OK and the money he wired us allowed Bertha to fly back to LA and begin the move. I began to realize that no matter what the situation is that you're going through in life, God can and will bless you if you stand on His Word.

Before Bertha left for LA, I promised her I'd look for a job. She said OK, but told me not to get a commission job. I looked in the newspaper and saw an interesting ad for employment. I called about it and went for an interview. It was a 100%

commission job selling home security systems. At the time, I didn't see any other jobs that interested me, so I took it. What I liked about the job was if I did the job properly, I wouldn't be making cold calls. I hated cold calling.

Bertha was not a happy camper after she returned to Delaware and found that I was working a 100% commission job. But I was making money. Without going into detail, I could sell very well, which I knew from my selling Microsoft Certified Systems Engineer training days. I also could train people and I became a unit manager. I grew my team, and began to manage other teams. From the day I first got the commission job, I began to walk around Mom's kitchen early in the morning, just like I did at 3719 Mt. Vernon Dr, praying to God for his blessings regarding this job and direction in my life during this season of my life.

When May 6, 2000 came around, I took my wife to New York City, to celebrate our 5 year wedding anniversary. We stayed at a nice hotel, browsed around the city, and took in a Broadway show. We took a 4 hour double-decker bus tour from 34th St. near the Empire State building, down past the World Trade Center to Battery Park. We boarded a tour boat to the Statue of Liberty, went inside the statue, than back on the tour bus to Central Park, then up to Harlem. From Harlem we went downtown back to 34th St. It was a very enjoyable tour and the tour operator, being very knowledgeable, made it very interesting. Of course, we didn't know that in 15 months the Twin Towers of the World Trade Center would be struck by terrorists and would be no more.

In the middle May, Bertha and I were still living with Mom in the house I lived in until I was 18 years old. As many women will attest to, it's difficult to have two women in the same kitchen. As loving as my mother always was, and as loving as Bertha can be, there was tension in the home. So, I got an apartment within walking distance to Mom's and the three of us were happy. It got to the point where Mom & Bertha would just hang out together. They became road buddies. This was very easy for Bertha because Bertha has always been a care-giver.

In June of 2000, I was essentially promoted to assistant manager of the Wilmington office of this home security systems company. We were in competition with the Main office and in August 2000, for the first time, our office had more security system installs than the Main office. I was making some serious money and I was told to search out a location for my own office. The revenue generated was so serious that the branch manager made $200,000 for the year 2000, and I quite honestly was the driving force of his success. I still remember how he and I talked and he was astounded at the money he made and he said he was saving all of it for a down payment on a new house.

Year 2001

I don't remember when, but our branch manager was able to buy his new home and I had the same thoughts too. Many of you have heard the saying, "when God starts blessing, the devil starts messing". The president of the company and I started looking for a location for my new office, and we found one in the outskirts of Newark, about 15 minutes from my apartment. In February, I moved into the new office and that's when the devil started messing. In the Wilmington office where I started out, the branch manager's job was to train and motivate the commission staff. He didn't go out in the field to sell. Well, the president of the company changed the rules in March and I was told I had to sell, as well as train and motivate the commission staff. All the time he and I were searching out locations, he never mentioned that I was going to have to sell. I was already working 12-14 hour days Monday—Friday, and I thought this added request was over the top. Towards the end of March, I was told that if I didn't produce any sales over that particular weekend, on Monday morning, the Vice President would be there to get my office keys and I could leave the company or go back to the Wilmington office. I went back to the Wilmington office for about a week and then I left the company.

Here I am again, not being able to generate revenue. I don't remember what I did in terms of looking for a job. But it was about to get reinforced in me again, that my God supplies all our need, according to his riches in glory by Christ Jesus.

Bertha had started working at Super Fresh, a large grocery store, the early part of 2001 as a cashier. It took her about 3 minutes to walk to work from our apartment. What Bertha had also done was to get her Delaware Residential Real Estate license. Due to her mortgage licensing that she had in California, she didn't need to take the National Real Estate exam in Delaware. All she needed to do was to study for and pass the Delaware State portion of the real estate exam to get a Delaware Resident Sales Real Estate license. So she took the exam and passed it. In Delaware, if you want to sell residential real estate, you have to affiliate with a licensed real estate broker in the state. Bertha placed her license with Weichert Realtors out of the Wilmington office. While working at Super Fresh and being a cashier, Bertha met a lot of people. Bertha became friends with this one particular customer who mentioned to Bertha that she was thinking about selling her house. In May 2001, Bertha got her first listing with this person and a few weeks later, her seller accepted on offer. Bertha's commission was about $3,700.

In June, I decided to get my real estate license, but classes didn't start until September. I remember going to class the first day, but the second day we got out about 10:30AM. I stopped by Super Fresh to see Bertha and I remember another cashier said that a plane had hit the World Trade Center. I go home and turned on the TV and I sat there in amazement at what I'm seeing. Both towers had been struck and after a while one tower collapsed followed by the other. My heart sank and I began to pray.

In December, I took the Delaware Residential Sales exam and passed it. I also learned that all I had to do to get a Pennsylvania Residential Sales license was to take the Pennsylvania State exam. I was already in the study mode, so I took the exam and passed it. In January 2002, I started selling real estate in Delaware and Pennsylvania. In April of 2002, I told Bertha to quit the Super Fresh job and we started working full time together in the real estate business as The Toulson Group. It was reinforced in me again that God is faithful and that by being obedient, God will bless you.

Victory Christian Fellowship Church

Going back to the end of 1999 and my Dad's death, Bertha and I had been attending the church where I attended until I was 18 years old, where I attended every Sunday with Mom & Dad. This was the church that Mom's mother and father attended, along with Mom's other sisters. So, there was still a lot of our family at the church when Bertha & I began attending with Mom in November 1999. Interestingly, the church hadn't changed that much. The format of the church service seemed the same to me, as well as the songs that were sung. When Bertha would want to share the hymnal book with me, I said I didn't need it because I still remembered the words to most of the songs. We were taking care of Mom now, and this is where we attended church.

Bertha was out shopping one day in a Wal-mart and she noticed a beauty salon inside of the Wal-mart. She went in to get her hair done. The lady who was doing her hair mentioned to Bertha Victory Christian Fellowship Church, so we went there the next Sunday. We enjoyed the service and I was impressed by the pastor, Gary V. Whetstone. So, we attended the following Sunday and every Sunday after that. Praise and Worship started promptly at 8:30AM and the church service started at 9 and was usually over around 10:30. At the end of this service, we'd rush to Mom's house and take her to her church. We probably did this for a year. The problem I was having with going to two services each Sunday was that I couldn't keep my eyes open at Mom's church. It was getting embarrassing. We normally sat on the second row, less than 10 feet from the alter. I tried everything to stay awake, but nothing worked.

In January 2002, I began to sell real estate and doing open houses. I could take Mom to church, but I couldn't stay. In my place, Bertha would take Mom to church. Over time however, Bertha would take Mom to church and various family members would bring her home. Either Bertha or I would take Mom to church every Sunday.

Spiritual Growth at Victory

A few pages ago, I mentioned that we joined Victory Christian Fellowship and, "the first of many shoots brought on by my seed of faith that began to grow in 1995, broke through good ground". When you plant a seed of corn or an apple seed, the first sign of growth that you see is the blade of the cornstalk or the soon to be trunk of the apple tree, which are also called shoots. The good ground that was mentioned was me. I've noted this scripture earlier in this writing, but it bares repeating again in the context of my spiritual growth. Mark 4: 3-20 reads:

3 Hearken; Behold, there went out a sower to sow: 4 And it came to pass, as he sowed, some fell by the way side, and the fowls of the air came and devoured it up. 5 And some fell on stony ground, where it had not much earth; and immediately it sprang up, because it had no depth of earth: 6 But when the sun was up, it was scorched; and because it had no root, it withered away. 7 And some fell among thorns, and the thorns grew up, and choked it, and it yielded no fruit. 8 And other fell on good ground, and did yield fruit that sprang up and increased; and brought forth, some thirty, and some sixty, and some an hundred. 9 And he said unto them, He that hath ears to hear, let him hear. 10 And when he was alone, they that were about him with the twelve asked of him the parable. 11 And he said unto them, Unto you it is given to know the mystery of the kingdom of God: but unto them that are without, all these things are done in parables: 12 That seeing they may see, and not perceive; and hearing they may hear, and not understand; lest at any time they should be converted, and their sins should be forgiven them. 13 And he said unto them, Know ye not this parable? and how then will ye know all

parables? 14 The sower soweth the word. 15 And these are they by the way side, where the word is sown; but when they have heard, Satan cometh immediately, and taketh away the word that was sown in their hearts. 16 And these are they likewise which are sown on stony ground; who, when they have heard the word, immediately receive it with gladness; 17 And have no root in themselves, and so endure but for a time: afterward, when affliction or persecution ariseth for the word's sake, immediately they are offended. 18 And these are they which are sown among thorns; such as hear the word, 19 And the cares of this world, and the deceitfulness of riches, and the lusts of other things entering in, choke the word, and it becometh unfruitful. 20 And these are they which are sown on good ground; such as hear the word, and receive it, and bring forth fruit, some thirtyfold, some sixty, and some an hundred.

As I mentioned earlier in this writing, prior to 1995, I was in the category of folks that Jesus talked about in verses 7 and 18-19. I really don't mean to be boastful, but I believe I am now good ground (verse 20), only by God's grace and His mercy in my life.

While faith was preached to me a Crenshaw Christian Center in Los Angeles, as in "faith cometh by hearing and hearing from the Word of God", my faith resulted in action at Victory Christian Fellowship. As the Word of God says, "faith without works is dead".

In 2000 when we joined Victory, I noticed right away that there were over 80 areas of ministry at the church. Crenshaw had several areas of ministries, but no where near 80. I was curious as to how these ministries got started. One Sunday morning, Pastor Faye Whetstone, wife of Pastor Gary, mentioned that anyone who felt they had a call on their life to reach out to the Body of Christ could submit an outline of what they wanted to do. This outline would be brought before the church leadership who would review the request. If the leadership felt this was a worthwhile ministry based on the outline and the outline met other church criteria, the ministry was granted. Some of the ministries are as follows:

A Ray of Hope – Ministry for those who have experienced the loss of a loved one.

Domestic Violence Ministry – a ministry for women of domestic violence, emotional, physical and verbal abuse.

Freedom Ministry – Ministry support for those desiring freedom from homosexuality. By appointment only.

Breaking the Yoke Ministry – Freedom from alcohol and substance abuse through God's healing power.

"WE CARE" HIV/AIDS Ministry – For persons affected by HIV/AIDS and their families.

Various Youth and Children's Ministries

Women's Ministry – a prayer, praise & worship fellowship for ALL Ladies.

Men of Change Ministry - A ministry designed to give practical solutions to difficult issues men face daily. This will be accomplished through biblical teachings combined with group discussion, prayer, and fellowship.

Marriage Fellowship - A ministry where married couples come together for an evening that will enrich their marriage. Each meeting is designed for a time of teaching, discussion, prayer, and fellowship.

I am an active part of The Men of Change Ministry which meets each Monday at 7PM. Bertha and I play a leadership role in the Marriage Fellowship which meets the first Friday of each month. This is one of our monthly date nights, and we clear our calendar for First Friday.

Spiritual Growth Year 2002

At Victory, Pastor Gary had talked about the Gary Whetstone Worldwide Ministries School of Biblical Studies program, and how the school was impacting lives in the US and many countries around the world. In 2002, my faith was still growing and I wanted a deeper and clearer understanding of God's Word. So I took action. I enrolled Bertha and me in the School of Biblical Studies and we started in September 2002. Since we were in our own business, the business allowed us to set our own schedule, so we decided to take the day class, (as opposed to an evening class), which was from 9AM to 12 Noon, Monday thru Friday. With permission from Dr. Gary V. Whetstone, my pastor, here is what is written as an overview of the School of Biblical Studies on his web-site at www.gwwm.com.

"God's plan for the School of Biblical Studies and the School of Ministerial Training began in the fall of 1984 when He spoke to Dr. Gary Whetstone to open a Bible School that would train the Body to become effective ministers of God's Word. During much time of prayer and observation of other Bible Schools around the country, vision and objectives were established so that you, as a believer, will receive the accurate, rightly divided

Word of Truth.

The purpose of these intensive courses of study is to enable you to live successfully in every area of your life and to empower you to reach those around you with the power of God's Word. Whether you attend for the purpose of full-time ministry or to promote personal growth, the curricula will equip you to advance the Kingdom of God both in a lost and dying world and in the Body of Christ".

We graduated on June 12, 2004 from the School of Biblical Studies. Bertha had the highest GPA of the 2004 class, and I wasn't far behind her. I inquired at Chesapeake Bible College & Seminary in Ridgely, MD and Bertha and I could have taken our credits from the School of Biblical Studies to Chesapeake Bible College & Seminary and received Associates Degrees in Biblical Studies. In fact, with Bertha's Pepperdine degree, she could have received a BA degree in Biblical Studies, and if I took 4 additional courses, I also could have received a BA in Biblical Studies. We didn't see the necessity to acquire the degrees, so we didn't pursue them.

The time we spent in Bible School was the most exciting and thought provoking time in my Christian walk. Early in Bible School, when it came to the day of exams, I found myself getting up around 4AM and studying to 6AM, going back to bed and getting up around 7:30AM. I did this all through the two years of Bible School. When Bible School was over, I continued to get up some mornings at 4AM to pray and read Proverbs for whatever day it was. For example, if it was the 5th of the month, I'd read Proverbs Chapter 5 or if it was the 20th of the month, I'd read Chapter 20. Eventually, before the Year 2004 was over, I was getting up every morning to pray and read Proverbs. Soon after that, Bertha would occasionally get up with me and we'd pray and read together.

Spiritual Growth Year 2003

Bertha and I attended our first Marriage Advance sponsored by Victory Christian Fellowship, during the Valentine's Day weekend of 2003. Married couples came from all over the region to attend the Advance, which was held at the luxurious Grand Hotel in Ocean City, MD. Check-in time was 4PM that Friday, with the opening session scheduled for 8PM. At the Marriage Advance, couples learn to appreciate their spouse's contributions in their lives and it's a time of romance and impactive teaching. Sunday evening, back at Victory, couples can renew their wedding vows during the 6PM Church service. Wives are encouraged to wear their wedding gowns.

Something interesting happened to Bertha and me at the Advance. After the 8PM session Saturday evening, there was going to be dancing, and Bertha and I were looking forward to dancing. Just before the 8PM session ended, I get a tap on my shoulder from the husband of a young couple who had been sitting behind us. I had noticed this couple sitting behind us at other sessions, but I paid it no mind. They asked if they could speak with us privately in their hotel room. They said it would probably take no more than 15-20 minutes. This young couple was having marital issues before they came to the Advance and were still having issues at the Advance. Bertha and I listened and referenced our responses according to what the Word of God said about their issues. Two hours later, after many tears from this young married couple, we emerged from their hotel room hoping to get a little dancing in. The room where the dancing had been was locked and the lights were out.

For several weeks after the Advance we counseled this couple and they were able to resolve their issues and gain a deeper appreciation of each other. They went on to become the first of many spiritual sons and daughters to us.

A few weeks later, another married couple came to us that were having some marital issues. We met with them at their home and over the course of a few weeks helped them resolve their issues.

A couple of weeks after that a couple that had just recently started coming to the Marriage Fellowship had some marital issues and they came to us. A few weeks later, mostly having discussions over the phone, we helped them resolve their issues.

At this point, Bertha and I came to believe that the Holy Spirit was putting married folks with issues in our path. We felt humbled that the Holy Spirit counted us worthy that he would flow through us to meet the needs of these marriages. So, Bertha and I came to believe that we had a Marriage Ministry.

Restoration

In Joel 2:25, the Word of God says, "And I will restore to you the years that the locust hath eaten, the cankerworm, and the caterpillar, and the palmerworm, my great army which I sent among you".

I was about to be restored. Not because I asked or prayed for it, but because of God's Grace towards me.

As I mentioned before, when I moved to Los Angeles in 1995, I never thought I'd come back to live in Newark, Delaware. However, God's plan for your life may never be revealed to you until your NOW moment. My NOW moment was about to become a WOW moment. As Bertha would tell you, when I'm at a loss for words when God moves in my life, all I can say is WOW.

In the first paragraph of this writing, called George, In The Beginning, I mention I was "...unable to buy Christmas gifts for my four children (actually five children, but later for that) ...". Well, now is the time for that.

In 1964 at the age of 14, I had my first real girlfriend. We were boy-friend and girl-friend until I was 18 and we got married in August 1968. I had graduated high school in June 1968. I graduated on a Tuesday, applied for a job at the Chrysler Assembly Plant in Newark on Wednesday, and started working that Thursday.

At the age of 19 I began to be unfaithful to my young wife. I know I was very young and not yet matured, but whichever way you look at it, it was totally my fault. I left my wife in December 1969 for another woman, but after several months, I went back to my wife. I tried to make it work, but by this time the woman I left my wife for was pregnant, and my daughter was born in September 1970. In the early part of 1971, I left my wife again. In October 1971, my wife gave birth to my 2nd daughter, but my wife and I we were still separated. For Christmas 1971, my mother and I went to where my wife was living to see my newborn 2nd daughter and to bring Christmas gifts to her. At the house was my wife, her sister, her mother, and grandmother. All, but the grandmother, insulted me and my mother. I know and can understand the animosity towards me, but to insult my mother was uncalled for and my mother and I left. My wife told me later that she wanted nothing to do with me, she didn't want child support, and she didn't want me to be in the baby's life. I said "fine". The baby's name was Gebrette Ronnell Toulson. My name is George Ronald Toulson.

I married the woman I left my wife for and we had three children and I adopted my 2nd wife's daughter. Years went by and I essentially forgot about Gebrette. I would think about her from time to time, but I was living my own life. I had heard that my first wife had re-married, but I didn't know where she lived.

As mentioned before, I came back to Newark in 1999 because my Dad had died. I can remember my first wife's sister (my nemesis) stopped by to "pay her respects" to me and Mom, but I really think she wanted to see what I looked like and how I was doing. I can remember being at a bar in 1985 and this sister was there enjoying the fact that I and my 2nd wife had recently divorced. At my Mom's house, she causally mentioned that "Brette" had asked about me and she wanted to see me. I asked her where Brette lived and she said in Maryland. I said something like, "I'm here". Since that time, I thought I'd be in the super market or in some other store and I'd get a tap on the shoulder, turn around, and she'd be there. It didn't happen that way.

In April 2003, while at the Weichert Office in the computer room, I heard my name paged over the inter-com. I picked up the phone and heard, "Hello, this is Gebrette Miles. Do you know who I am"? I said, "Yes, I've been expecting you". I don't remember what else we talked about. We exchanged phone numbers and e-mail addresses. I got off the phone and went back to my office area where Bertha was sitting. She saw that I was visibly shaken and she asked me what had happened. I really felt weak in my knees and had to sit down. I told her that the call was from Gebrette. I told her about the conversation we had and that Gebrette and I were going to talk later that evening.

I called Gebrette later that evening, but I don't remember what we talked about. However, the conversation was very enjoyable for both of us. She told me that everybody calls her "Brette". I asked her how she came to find me and call me. She told me as a child, she remembered seeing a Charlie Brown book with her name written in it. It said Gebrette Toulson. She was young so she didn't really know what to make of it since that wasn't her last name (her mother had remarried), but she knew it meant something so it always stuck with her. So she always knew I existed, but she just filed it away in her mind.

Brette said she was traveling to Italy for a two-week study abroad trip and needed to get a passport. In order to do so, she needed her birth certificate, which is the first time she saw proof that I actually existed. She thinks that was in the fall of 1995 because she went to Italy in January 1996

Brette said her mom and aunt (my nemesis) started casually making mention of either seeing me in Newark or that people had seen me around town. You know how the small-town network works she said. So she knew I was back in Newark, although she didn't know I had moved away to California years before. Then, a cousin brought it to her mom's attention that I was in the paper in a Weichert Realtors ad. Brette was taking a real estate class at the time and had learned that you can look up any realtor by the state they are licensed in. So, one day at work she looked me up. She said she wasn't sure how long it was between the time she found my number and when she called me. Maybe a few days, or it may have been that same day.

Brette said that she was married, no kids, and lived in Hanover, MD. She had two Master's Degrees, one in Public Administration and the other in Health Services Administration. Her husband had two master's degrees as well. She said she and her husband had a strong Christian Faith. In our conversation, I mentioned that Bertha had to be in Baltimore the week-end after next to take the real estate exam to get her Maryland license. Brette invited us to stay at her house that weekend. After 32 years, I was going to be re-united with my daughter!

I'll always remember the day I walked up the sidewalk to her front door. They had a beautiful house. The door opened and there she was. She was beautiful and looked more like me than any of my other children. I can't express in writing how I felt, but I remembered thanking God for how I felt in him giving me back my daughter after 32 years. We spent Friday and Saturday night with them and returned to Newark late Sunday evening. We communicated by phone and e-mail everyday for several weeks.

Now that Brette and I had re-united after 32 years, how was I going to introduce her to her four siblings? I didn't want to tell the siblings individually over the phone, for I knew I'd tell one something and not tell the others. So, I decided to send a group e-mail. In the e-mail I laid out exactly what happened – the timeline, relationships, and all the unflattering details. I would have loved to have heard the siblings conversations. They were surprised to say the least, but I found out that the four siblings had heard some things about Brette and Brette heard some things about them. This wasn't hard to do, considering the ages and where the five went to high school. The high schools were no more than a 30 minute ride from each other. Demetria was born in 1968, Angie 1970, Gebrette 1971, George, Jr 1972, and Charles 1973. Demetria, Angie, and Charles went to Sanford, George went to Tatnall and Brette went to Newark High School. Sanford was ranked in the top three high school basketball programs in Delaware, and Charles was a starter. George was a football star at Tatnall, the #1 ranked scholastically school in Delaware. So, it wasn't inconceivable that they heard about each other.

Angie, who was visiting Bertha and me from Erie, PA where she lived with her husband and my three grandchildren, was down the weekend after receiving the e-mail. Brette called me while Angie was at my apartment. Angie said she wanted to talk to her so I gave the phone to Angie and left the room. But I stood outside the door and listened to the conversation. After a minute or so, I heard Angie laughing, and I was relieved. Brette came up the next day and she and Angie were just beaming at one another. Brette's other siblings met her eventually and you'd never know that they just met. Brette fit right in with her siblings. All five of my children, young adults at this point, were college graduates. Angie and Charles were medical doctors, and George, Jr had several advanced financial designations.

The weekend that Brette came up to met Angie, was the weekend she met Mom for the first time since Christmas 1971. I re-introduced Mom to her granddaughter. Mom could certainly see the likeness of Brette in me. Mom and I had a long talk about Brette and she was very happy to have another granddaughter. On many occasions after that, Brette would stop by on her own to talk to Mom, who she called Grand Mom.

For Thanksgiving 2003, Brette invited her re-united family down to her house for Thanksgiving dinner. There were several times when all five grand children were at Mom's house. Where do you begin to thank God for this blessed event? For me, my words were inadequate. Of the many things I know about God, I am the evidence of God's faithfulness to those who believe! And I know that God will restore all of this and more!

Spiritual Growth 2004

In March 2004, Bertha and I heeded the call for performers for the upcoming Passion Play at Victory Christian Fellowship. Neither one of us had acted in a play before, so we were excited to be a part of this ministry to the Body of Christ. I believe there were 14-16 performances. I played one of 12 disciples and a Sadducee in all the performances. Bertha played Satan in the Garden of Gethsemane scene. She was dressed in all black with a hood, with white face paint, on an iridescent lighted stage. She was menacing and scary! In fact, the director of the play, kept her isolated from the rest of the cast, in order to keep her in character. The other play characters wanted nothing to do with her. This play would be performed again in March 2005, but this time not only would I be a disciple, but I'd also play the part of Pontius Pilate as well.

At the end of each performance, anyone in the audience who had not accepted Jesus Christ as their Lord and Savior was offered the opportunity to give their life to Christ and become part of the Body of Christ. There were close to one thousand people that gave their life to Christ as a result of the Passion Play.

This play was very uplifting for me because the director made all the cast members think about what we were portraying and the necessity for each performer to stay in character throughout the play.

It was also a time where I gained a 2nd spiritual son who played a disciple along side of me. One day during rehearsal, he started calling me "Dad". I didn't question him as to why he was calling me "Dad". But I did inquire later, discreetly, about his father, who I was told was deceased. Therefore, I started to call him "Son".

Our First Sermons

As previously mentioned, Bertha and I graduated from the School of Biblical Studies at the Gary Whetstone Worldwide Ministries in June 2004. A final requirement for graduation was to give a 20 minute sermon. Bertha's abbreviated sermon is below (3 pg). It's awesome! Mine will follow (2 pg).

CHAPTER 11
BERTHA'S SERMON

WHAT ARE YOU THINKING ABOUT

Thoughts

"Thoughts" are defined by Webster's Dictionary as the product of mental activity, consideration, attention, judgment, opinion, regard. We can have good thoughts or bad thoughts – Thoughts that foster life or brings death. We are to decide. Proverbs 23:7 says as a man thinks in his heart, so is he. We are also told in Deut 30:19, "I call heaven and earth to record this day against you, that I have set before you life and death, blessing and cursing: therefore choose life, that both thou and thy seed may live". Choosing life, we need to ask ourselves moment by moment - WHAT ARE YOU THINKING ABOUT?

Controlling our thought life is done with offensive and defensive strategies: Pulling down strongholds, casting down imaginations; then renewing our minds. If this sounds like fighting, that's because it is. Thoughts come to us all the time. If we allow them, the same ugly thoughts will come time after time, like a New York Ticker Tape circling around and around with information on the stock market . Thoughts will come over and over and over again until we become so familiar with them that they form strongholds in our minds. (Webster defines "stronghold" as 1. well-fortified place; 2. a place that serves as the center of a faction or of any group sharing certain opinion and attitudes). With the passing of certain events, the thoughts you entertain will be vocalized or acted out. Strongholds – For example, someone offends you when they do or say something. The thought comes to your mind of what you would like to do the next time this happens; You didn't act on it, you just thought it. Unless you cast that thought down and replace it with the Word, you will say what you planned in your mind to say the next time the circumstances present themselves. You see, we must take corrective action over our thoughts, if not, we will embarrass ourselves, hurt someone else and thereby disqualify ourselves as Christian witnesses. I ask you, WHAT ARE YOU THINKING ABOUT?

The thought comes to you, "Do I have cancer"? Where did that come from? Satan? Possibly. Certainly not God! Get into your fighting posture. Cast down the thought immediately (Webster defines "cast" as 1. to throw or hurl; 3. to cause to fall; 6. to shed or drop), then come back with the replacement action. The Word of God in Isa 53:5 says, "But he was wounded for my transgressions, he was bruised for my iniquities: the chastisement of my peace was upon him: and with his stripes I am healed". What about, "are my children going to hell"? Grab that thought like you are wrestling a burglar, bind it and cast it down. Here comes corrective action. Psalm 138:8 says, "The Lord will perfect that which concerneth me: thy mercy, O Lord, endureth forever: forsake not the works of thine own hands". James 5:16 says, "…The effectual fervent prayer of a righteous man availeth much". II Tim 1:7 says, "For God has not given me the spirit of fear; but of power, of love, and of a sound mind".

Have you ever wondered what would cause a person to commit the crime of murder? We gasp when hearing the news that a husband killed his wife; A mother drowned her children; The act of murder started with a thought. The thought was planted long before the action ever took place. When we think hateful thoughts, the scripture says we have committed murder already in our hearts. When discussing the subject of adultery, the bible says in Matthew 5:27-28, "Ye have heard that it was said by them of old time, Thou shalt not commit adultery: Vs 28: But I say unto you that whosoever looketh on a woman to lust after her hath committed adultery with her already in his heart". There is no such thing as it was an accident. It had happened in his heart, which came by way of his thought life.

I have stood by the refrigerator and tried to eat something though I was not hungry. Why was I standing there then if I weren't hungry? Satan? Maybe, but I am the one who has to take responsibility. Have you looked at a commercial on TV and all of a sudden you got hungry? Many times you wanted the exact thing you saw on the commercial. Advertising? Yes, but I am in control.

We never "arrive". Some pastors have thought they arrived only to find themselves in trouble with the law or in adultery which caused the church family to suffer in addition to their own family.

What Influences Our Thoughts

It depends if you are walking in the flesh or in the spirit. Galatians 5:16-26 says, "... Walk in the Spirit, and ye shall not fulfill the lust of the flesh. Vs 17: For the flesh lusteth against the Spirit, and the Spirit against the flesh: and these are contrary the one to the other: so that ye cannot do the things that ye would. Vs 18: But if ye be led by the Spirit, ye are not under the law. Vs 19: Now the works of the flesh are manifest, which are these; Adultery, fornication, uncleanness, lasciviousness, Vs 20: Idolatry, witchcraft, hatred, variance, emulations, wrath, strife, seditions, heresies, Vs 21: Envyings, murders, drunkenness, revellings and such like: of the which I tell you before, as I have also told you in time past, that they which do such things shall not inherit the kingdom of God. Vs 22: But the fruit of the Spirit is love, joy, peace, longsuffering, gentleness, goodness, faith, Vs 23: Meekness, temperance: against such there is no law. Vs 24: And they that are Christ's have crucified the flesh with the affections and lusts. Vs 25: If we live in the Spirit, let us also walk in the Spirit. Vs 26: Let us not be desirous of vain glory, provoking one another and envying one another. So, WHAT ARE YOU THINKING ABOUT?

How Do We Control Our Thoughts

Thoughts can come from a variety of sources: In our study on the four sources of wisdom, we learned that thoughts come from God, Satan, our own senses, and from the world. Like a computer, we have to program our minds with the right information, so that we are not left with the negative consequences in life of acting inappropriately, living beneath our blessed inheritance or something worse.

How do we program the right information to our minds? The Bible tells us to renew our minds; Romans 12:1-3 says "I beseech you therefore brethren, by the mercies of God, that ye present your bodies a living sacrifice, holy, acceptable unto God, which is your reasonable service. Vs 2: And be not conformed to this world: but be ye transformed by the renewing of your mind, that ye may prove what is that good, and acceptable, and perfect, will of God. Vs 3: For I say, through the grace given unto me, to every man that is among you, not to think of himself more highly than he ought to think; but to think soberly, according as God hath dealt to every man the measure of faith". Renewing the mind is a process which is attentive to each detail of every thought. Thoughts have to pass an acid test before they should be allowed to lodge in our minds. Philippians 4:8 says "Finally, brethren, whatsoever things are true, whatsoever things are honest, whatsoever things are just, whatsoever things are pure, whatsoever things are lovely, whatsoever things are of good report; if there be any virtue, and if there be any praise, think on these things". Something may be true, but if it does not meet the other requirements of this scripture, like if there is no virtue or praise in it, the thought is not allowed. So I ask you, **WHAT ARE YOU THINKING ABOUT?**

Thoughts come to us like missiles all day long. We should have the "whole armor of God on" including our helmet of salvation, which would deflect the thought. But if the thought comes anyway, we have the Word of God to quench every fiery dart of the wicked one. Joshua 1:8 says, "This book of the law shall not depart out of thy mouth; but thou shalt meditate therein day and night, that thou mayest observe to do according to all that is written therein: for then thou shalt make thy way prosperous and then thou shalt have good success".

My husband George and I wake up early in the morning to spend time in prayer and the reading of God's Word. This daily exercise builds us up in our spirit man and our soul. We are told in III John 1:2, "Beloved, I wish above all things that thou mayest prosper and be in health, even as thy soul prospereth". God wants us to prosper in all areas of our lives. He wants us happy. God's Word changes our thoughts and conforms them to His thoughts. We then glorify God and bless our fellow man.

God cares about everything that concerns us. He desires to fellowship with us. In Psalm 35:27 – 28 it says "Let them shout for joy and be glad, that favor my righteous cause: yea, let them say continually, Let the Lord be magnified, which has pleasure in the prosperity of his servant. Vs 28: And my tongue shall speak of thy righteousness and of thy praise all the day long".

Conclusion

Mankind was created to enjoy fellowship with God. We worship God in spirit and in truth. God's Word is His truth. The unrenewed mind is governed by the flesh. Flesh is diametrically opposed to the spirit. Our joy, happiness and prosperity are dependent on our walking in the spirit and continually taking authority over our thoughts. "For though we walk in the flesh, we do not war after the flesh". Renewing our minds is a constant process. George and I worship and praise God early in the morning, reading the scriptures which reinforce our Christian walk. We can laugh and enjoy fellowship with God and other people. George and I are not anxious or intimidated. We think no evil, therefore we speak no evil. We have joy, we have love, and that love affects and infects people around us. So, WHAT ARE YOU THINKING ABOUT? We are thinking about God! And behaving like Him. After all, He is Our Father.

George's Abbreviated Sermon

I've had several occasions where I've ministered this abbreviated sermon to a non-believer. I've not always been successful in having them give their life to Christ, but I enjoyed the effort. I think the Holy Spirit was clever in how he gave this sermon to me to minister to a non-believer. This abbreviated sermon is only 2 pages long. I hope you appreciate and enjoy it.

How Long is Eternity?

How long is eternity? In Isaiah 57:15, the prophet writes "For thus says the High and Lofty one Who inhabits eternity, whose name is Holy: ...". So we know that eternity exists. One of Webster's Dictionary definitions of Eternity is: the timeless state into which the soul is believed to pass at death.

Is there a heaven and a hell where you might spend eternity? The bible certainly declares YES to both questions. In fact, based on the Strong's Exhaustive Concordance of the Bible, there are 582 references of the word "heaven" and only 54 references of the word "hell". It should be interesting to ponder the question, "why are there 10 times as many references to "heaven" as to "hell"?

Let me ask this question another way. "Is there a heaven and a hell where you might spend eternity"? Let's address this question from a practical point of view. Let's look at the odds. Most people know what odds are. In horse racing, 20 to 1 odds are considered a long shot. This means that the maker of the odds is saying that they give a certain horse 1 chance in 20 races to win. Conversely, 2 to 1 odds means a given horse is given 1 chance in 2 races to win. This is the closest thing to "a sure thing". If you throw dice, you can understand how you have 1 chance or outcome in 6, to roll a given number. What about the various state lotteries, where the odds of winning the big bucks are at least a couple of million to 1? Somewhere I heard the new American Dream was to win the lottery.

A few of you may say, "I don't believe there is a heaven or a hell". Keep in mind something. It doesn't matter what you believe! Again, let's look at the odds. There are only 3 chances or outcomes of the question, whether there is a heaven or hell. One chance is Yes, one chance is No, and a third chance is there is Neither a heaven or hell. You have 3 to 1 odds as the odds makers call it. Those of you who have ever gambled and those of you who have never gambled should understand my point. With 3 to 1 odds, why run the risk of going to hell? Webster defines hell as: 1) the place or state of punishment of the wicked after death; the abode of evil or condemned spirits. 2) any place or state of torment or misery. 3) the abode of the dead; Sheol or Hades.

Jesus was known to give many parables when teaching. A parable is defined as short-story designed to illustrate or teach some truth, religious principle or lesson. In the gospel of Luke 16:19-31, Jesus tells a story or a truth. This is not a parable. This is a statement of fact from our Lord and Savior. Jesus talks about 2 people who are going to spend eternity in two different places. Read bible verses. Notice in these scriptures, that torment is mentioned four times. Webster defines torment as: 1) to afflict with great, usually incessant or repeated bodily or mental suffering. 2) a state of great bodily or mental suffering; agony; misery. In verse 23 Read bible verse. In verse 24, Read bible verse. In verse 25, Read bible verse. In verses 27-28, Read bible verse.

So, for the last time, I'll ask the question, how long is eternity? Again, let's look at it from a practical point of view. A well know bible scholar and teacher gave an example of eternity's time measure that will be helpful in our thinking. Bear with me as I throw some rather large numbers at you, but they are necessary to make the point. The earth's sun is 93 million miles from earth, while the earth's moon is 240,000 miles from earth. The fastest measure of speed that man can actually calculate is the speed of light. Light speed is 186,000 miles per second, or 11,160,000 miles per hour. For light to travel from the earth to the surface of the moon, would take 1.29 seconds. For light to travel from the earth to the sun, would take 8.33 minutes. Now imagine all the grains of sand, on all the beaches of the earth. Can you picture that? Also imagine an eagle taking one grain of sand and flying to the sun. Now you know the eagle doesn't fly at 11,160,000 miles per hour. Can you picture that? Once the eagle deposits the grain of sand at the sun, he flies back to earth to get another grain of sand. The eagle does this until all the grains of sand, on all the beaches of the earth, have been deposit at the sun. This, the biblical scholar submits to you, is One Day in eternity. Again I ask this question. With 3 to 1 odds that there is a hell, why take the risk?

As I mentioned previously, Strong's Exhaustive Concordance has 582 occurrences of the word "heaven" and 54 occurrences of the word "hell". The word "heaven" is mentioned in 53 of the 66 books of the bible. Thirty-two books of the Old Testament and 21 books of the New Testament. From Genesis' "In the beginning, God created the heavens and the earth ...", to

Malachi, where God is speaking, "If I will not open for you the windows of heaven and pour you out such blessing that there will not be room enough to receive it …", to the seven parables in Matthew, where Jesus says "…the kingdom of heaven is like a man who sows good seed in his field", "… the kingdom of heaven is like a mustard seed …", "…the kingdom of heaven is like leaven…", …the kingdom if heaven is like a treasure hidden in a field…", "the kingdom of heaven is like merchant seeking a beautiful pearl…", "… the kingdom of heaven is like a dragnet that was cast into the sea …" to the Book of Revelation, "Now I saw a new heaven and new earth, for the first heaven and the first earth had passed away."

Of the 54 references of "hell", it is mentioned in 10 books of the Old Testament and 7 books of the New Testament. I'll use the one text in which Jesus said, "And this I say to you, that you are Peter, and on this rock I will build my church and the gates of hell (or Hades) shall not prevail against it." As the bible clearly says, there is a heaven and a hell, and eternity awaits each and every one of us. In 2 Peter 3:8, it reads, 8 But, beloved, be not ignorant of this one thing, that one day is with the Lord as a thousand years, and a thousand years as one day.

I also let the unbeliever know that all that is required to make sure he or she goes to heaven and not hell is to speak and believe Romans 10:9-10.

At Victory Christian Fellowship, we've been taught to ask a very simply question to each and everyone. The question is, "if you should die at this very moment, do you know for certain that you would wake up in the throne room of God"? If the answer is NO, we lead them to salvation using Romans 10:9-10.

In 2004, with the completion and graduation from bible school, I am extremely proud of Bertha's and my accomplishment. I particularly want my faith and my actions to go beyond what I've learned. I want more of the Word of God and I want to see the manifestations of His Word. I remembered the scriptures that Pastor Jimmy Price gave me in 1997 and I began to pray the Word and I wrote this prayer using Pastor Jimmy's scriptures.   The prayer is entitled Spiritual Foundation Prayer.

Spiritual Foundation Prayer

Father, I thank you for sustaining us.

Father, I thank you for allowing us to abide under your shadow.

Father, I thank you that you are faithful.

Father, I thank you that all of my need is met, according to your riches in glory by Christ Jesus.

I thank you Dear God that I am focused on the promises that are in Deuteronomy 28:1-14 and not the circumstances:

I will not be moved by how I feel or don't feel, for those are circumstances and distractions.

I will not be moved by what I see or don't see, for those are circumstances and distractions.

I will not be moved by what I hear or don't hear, for those

are circumstances and distractions.

I am only moved by the Spirit of the Living God!

I thank you Dear God that no weapon formed against me, my wife, or our family shall prosper, and every tongue that rises up in judgment against us, we shall condemn.

I thank you Dear God that you have not given me the spirit of fear, but the spirit of power, and of love, and of a sound mind.

Regarding not being moved by the circumstances above, many of the circumstances we face in life deal with the senses or our flesh. Feeling is emotional such as anger or bitterness, while seeing and hearing are two of the five senses. How do you know when you are focused on the promises as opposed to the circumstances? While you have tears streaming down your face because of how you feel or don't feel, or when you see something with your eyes or you don't see something that you expected to see, or when you hear something you didn't want to hear, or when you didn't hear something you expected to hear, can you speak with your mouth and say, "I will not be moved by (the circumstances). I am only moved by the Spirit of the Living God". I believe your speaking with your mouth notifies the circumstances that you will not be moved by them. I believe your human spirit is using your month to proclaim victory over the circumstances. I believe these circumstances are distracting you from the Word of God. I further believe you're going to have to use your faith in God to go through the circumstances, not over them, not around them, not under them, but through them.

Looking back over the courses we took during the two years of the School of Biblical Studies, my two favorite courses were "Holy Spirit" and "Victory In Spiritual Warfare". I would venture to say that most spirit-filled believers don't understand that we as Christians are in some kind of spiritual warfare everyday. The warfare most likely won't be a knock down, drag out, in your face type of fight, although it could be, as a fight against sickness or disease, or your marriage. However, you know that "stuff" is coming against you, your wife, or your family. In some situations, the fight will be ever so subtle, so much so that you don't even know you're in a fight. Regarding spiritual warfare, the Holy Spirit put on my heart to write this prayer. This prayer was developed over several months of unctions from the Holy Spirit, where I wrote down every unction I received.

Spiritual Warfare Prayer

Father, I thank you for your Word, for your Word is truth and your Word is life, and it will not return unto you void, but will accomplish your divine decree. (Isaiah 55:11)

Father, I thank you that your Word declares that greater is He that lives in me then he that is in the world. (1 John 4:4)

Father, I thank you that at the Name of Jesus, every knee shall bow and every tongue shall confess that Jesus is Lord! (Romans 14:11)

Father, I thank you that your Word declares that I am above only and not beneath, that I am the head and not the tail, that I have right standing. (Deuteronomy 28: 13)

Father, I thank you that your Word declares that whatsoever I bind on earth is bound in heaven, and whatsoever I loose on earth is loosed in heaven.
(Matthew 16: 19)

Therefore Satan, you and your demon spirits, I come against you with the same Holy Spirit Power (I'm a spirit-filled believer) that raised Jesus from the dead. You have no authority over me, my wife, or our families in the Name of Jesus.

Satan, you and your demon spirits, the Word of God says that greater is He that lives in me than he that is in the world.

Satan, you and your demon spirits, the Word of God says that I am above only and not beneath, that I am the head and not the tail, that I have right standing.

Satan, you and your demon spirits, the Word of God says that whatsoever I bind on earth is bound in heaven, and whatsoever I loose on earth is loosed in heaven.

Therefore Satan, you and your demon spirits, I bind and rebuke all of your financial maneuvers and strategies against me, my wife and our families in the Name of Jesus, and I command you to loose all of your financial assignments against me, my wife, and our families in the Name of Jesus!

Satan, you and your demon spirits, I bind and rebuke all of your business maneuvers and strategies against me, my wife and our families in the Name of Jesus, and I command you to loose all of your business assignments against me, my wife, and our families in the Name of Jesus!

Satan, you and your demon spirits, I bind and rebuke all of your legal maneuvers and strategies against me, my wife and our families in the Name of Jesus, and I command you to loose all of your legal assignments against me, my wife, and our families in the Name of Jesus!

Satan, you and your demon spirits, I bind and rebuke all of your marriage maneuvers and strategies against me, my wife and our families in the Name of Jesus, and I command you to loose all of your marriage assignments against me, my wife, and our families in the Name of Jesus!

Satan, you and your demon spirits, I bind and rebuke all of your personal maneuvers and strategies against me, my wife and our families in the Name of Jesus, and I command you to loose all of your personal assignments against me, my wife, and our families in the Name of Jesus!

Satan, you and your demon spirits, I bind and rebuke all of your mechanical maneuvers and strategies against me, my wife and our families in the Name of Jesus, and I command you to loose all of your mechanical assignments against me, my wife, and our families in the Name of Jesus!

Satan, you and your demon spirits, I bind and rebuke all of your health maneuvers and strategies against me, my wife and our families in the Name of Jesus, and I command you to loose all of your health assignments against me, my wife, and our families in the Name of Jesus!

Father, I thank you for loosing all of your ministering spirits to provide me, my wife and our families with all of our needs and desires in the Name of Jesus!

Let's focus on two points regarding this prayer and gain a deeper understanding of the power of the prayer. In marriage, first and foremost, we are under spiritual attack. God ordained two institutions – marriage and the church. Is it then any wonder why Satan comes against marriage so much and so strong? However, Jesus gave us examples of how to address Satan and his demon spirits.

Point # 1

After Jesus was baptized in the Jordan river, where the Holy Spirit came upon him, he was lead by the Holy Spirit into the wilderness to be tempted by Satan. When Satan came to Jesus, Jesus didn't argue with him or debate him, Jesus simply said "It is written...", essentially three times, and after the third time, Satan departed from him for a season (Luke 4:1-13). Jesus spoke the Word of God and Satan finally left him. In our prayer above, when we say, "the Word of God says ...", it's the same thing as Jesus saying, "It is written...".

Point # 2

In Mark 5: -13, the demon spirits that possess a man know Jesus and are afraid of him, as noted in verse 7. Jesus spoke to them. Therefore, because Jesus is our Lord and Savior, and we have His nature, we can speak to the demon spirits also, as noted in the above prayer.

Get this prayer into your spirit. I know this prayer will

fortify you in your marriage.

Spiritual Growth 2005

Aruba

In November 2004, I began to think about our 10 year wedding anniversary in May 2005. I wanted to do some things Bertha and I never did before to make our anniversary memorable. I've always liked the sound of Aruba so I went to a travel agent in Newark to inquire about Aruba. From Wikipedia, you find that Aruba is a country that is a 21 mile long island, about 17 miles north of Venezuela, with warm sunny weather, with little rain, all year long. The country is part of the Lesser Antilles and is governed by Kingdom of the Netherlands. I booked the travel and was able to pay with cash.

We arrived in Aruba on January 16, 2005 for a 7 day/6 night stay at the Holiday Inn Sun Spree Resort, Palm Beach. Our room was on the 6th floor overlooking the beautiful white sand beach with palm trees, and aqua colored waters of the Caribbean. I had my camcorder and captured all that could be seen from our balcony and the beach area near our hotel.

We were able to go on several excursions and the three most interesting were Scuba, Horse Back riding and the Thriller Power Boat ride.

With Scuba, you put on a heavy diving helmet with an air hose coming into the top of the helmet bringing in air to breathe and keeping water out. We then went under water down a ladder to about 25 feet, walked around and toured a sunken plane. They also had an underwater club with tables and chairs that you could actually sit on. They took pictures and provided us with a DVD of the underwater adventure.

For horse back riding, we went to a ranch that matched each rider with the appropriate sized horse. We then rode to the north side of the island, going uphill for a few miles. Upon getting to the top of the hill, you were rewarded with a spectacular view the Caribbean Sea. As we rode down the hill you could see that there were no beaches, just rocks that also made a spectacular scene as the Caribbean crashes against the rocks. I had my camcorder and was able to record as I rode. We stopped after awhile and some folks went swimming in an area that was deep enough to dive into. Arriving back at the ranch we eat lunch and took our tour bus back to the hotel.

The Thriller Power Boat Ride allows you to live the experience of real off-shore power boating. The boat could accommodate up to 40 passengers and could reach a top speed of 50 miles per hour. That was exciting!

We toured the island, did a little shopping, ate at nice restaurants and had the best time vacationing of our 10 years of marriage. Lying on the beach and in our hotel room, we reminisced over the 10 years, sometimes laughing and other times shaking our heads in acknowledgement of how God brought us through some very challenging times. I actually looked at the camcorder tape of our trip to Aruba for this writing, and at end of the tape, I'm thanking God for the vacation and celebration of our marriage.

CHAPTER 12
10 YEARS

On May 5, 2005, to actually celebrate our 10 year wedding anniversary (May 6th), Bertha and I took our first cruise together aboard the Carnival Legend out of New York City. It would be an 8 Day Southern Caribbean Cruise paid with cash. Bertha had been on cruises before, but this was my first. The two most important factors for me in booking the cruise were I wanted a balcony stateroom and I wanted to cruise out of New York City. It was exciting leaving the pier going down the Hudson River with Bertha. I pointed out to her where the Twin Towers of the World Trade Center once stood, and it was also exciting going past the Statue of Liberty. I wanted to be at sea for a few days, to experience the wonders of God, as opposed to flying to Miami and getting aboard a cruise ship. I purposely chose a port side (left side) stateroom of the ship because I wanted to see the sun rise over the ocean, which signified a new day that no man had seen before, and I wanted to thank God personally for seeing this new day. Our ports of call would be St. Thomas, San Juan and Tortola, and it would take us about 2 ½ days to get to our first port of call.

Bertha and I have always loved to get dressed up and a cruise ship is the perfect opportunity to do so. At dinner, we wore sharp casual clothes once, a tuxedo and gown once for the Captain's Ball, and the other four nights I wore a suit and tie and Bertha dresses. We had three other couples that ate with us during our 8PM dinner time. We enjoyed our dinner guests, dinner, and the Broadway type shows after dinner were sometimes the highlight of our day. We spent few bucks on photos, but it was well worth it.

At St. Thomas, we take a cable car to the top of the highest mountain and had a spectacular view of the island and three cruise ships that were docked below. Bertha's sisters Joyce and JoAnn came to St. Thomas on one of those cruise ships and we got a chance to talk with them and take some photos.

I brought my camcorder along and have about 2 hours of footage. For me there's always something special about doing something for the first time with Bertha. It's something we can talk and reminisce about. Having the camcorder tapes brings back the memories. This is the 2nd extraordinary blessing that God has bestowed on us in 2005, but He's not done yet!

Erie, PA

In June of 2005, Bertha and I went to Erie, PA to celebrate my first grandson's 2nd birthday, and the party was on a Saturday. Bill, my son-in-law and my daughter Angie, had put together a fun day for William, my grandson. We had additional family members and friends present. The interesting thing about this time is that Angie wanted to have church on Sunday, and she asked if I would give a sermon and Bertha would be the praise and worship leader. Of course we said Yes! Surprisingly to me, I wasn't nervous at all. In fact, I was excited to preach, actually teach, the Word God. I really enjoyed the praise and worship and I liked how the Holy Spirit flowed through me to bring God's Word to the family and friends in attendance. We had an exhilarating time and Angie enjoyed it so much she called it the *Erie Praise and Pool Fellowship*. The name came about because we had the church service outside by the swimming pool. We hoped to do it again later in the summer, but it didn't happen. I thanked God for giving me the opportunity to show members of my family a side of me that they never saw before. I know the experience strengthened my family.

Los Angeles

In the beginning of August, we went to Los Angeles for 7 days, staying at a Holiday Inn Express, within walking distance of Venice Beach. The trip was paid with cash. It was the first time I had been back to LA since I left in October 1999. I almost cried being back in LA. It was sunshine, blue skies, the ocean and the mountains. It was being at LAX watching the Boeing 747 jumbo jets take off and land. It was seeing family and friends that Bertha and I hadn't seen in several years.

One dear friend Gloria, who went to Jefferson High School with Bertha and her sister Joyce, gave us a day I'll always remember. Gloria and her husband Jimmy, took us on a day trip up to Santa Barbara, CA. We left their house in Woodland Hills, CA in the morning, went thru Topanga Canyon (breathtaking), to the Pacific Coast Highway, where the drive is beautiful, to Malibu, CA, where we did some sightseeing. As we were driving, we could see many homes in Malibu that were sitting on hills that looked out over the Pacific Ocean. We then went to Oxnard, than back on the Pacific Coast Highway to Santa Barbara, where we had lunch. From there we went to the Lake Cachuma Recreation Area and toured the lake. We got back to Gloria's house late afternoon. We had an absolute fantastic time that day, again, a day I'll always remember.

You might be asking yourself, how was this trip about spiritual growth? Bertha and I know where we've come from, and we know what we've gone through, before our marriage and during our marriage. If it were not for God's Grace and His Mercy, for God's Financial Grace and His Financial Mercy, we don't know where we'd be. We've had a fantastic year in 2005, and I believe that you the reader would agree. We owe it all to God. Our faith is growing deeper, because Bertha and I are the evidence of God's faithfulness. God is a God of abundance, and he was not done blessing us yet!

Israel & Jordan – The Best of the Holy Land Tour

Bertha and I were about to engage in the greatest time of our life, in going to Israel and Jordan – The Best of the Holy Land Tour. In the spring of 2005, Victory Christian Fellowship announced that the church was taking a trip to Israel, and Bertha and I decided that we'd go. It was a blessing that we were in the real estate business and as such could dictate our hours. The tour would be for 11 days, starting on September 13th and we'd return on September 23rd. The tour operator was Noseworthy Travel Services. The cost of the trip was $4,600 and was paid for with cash. We'd be flying out of New York's JFK airport on Royal Jordanian non-stop to Amman, Jordan, an 11 hour flight. We departed JFK at 11PM and arrived in Jordan the next day at 5PM. Prior to the trip, the church had three meetings to go over the itinerary, customs, and travel protocol. There would be 24 people in attendance, including Pastors Gary and Faye Whetstone.

Jordan

The first part of the trip would be a tour of the cities of Jerash and Petra and we'd end up at Mt. Nebo, where Moses would look over into the Promised Land, but not enter it. We would spend two full days in Jordan. We were escorted by an armed Jordanian guard at all times.

Jerash was a Roman city that was prosperous in the 1st and 2nd centuries A.D. The ruins of the city, which we toured, were in some cases surprisingly intact due to abandonment by subsequent ancient civilizations. Theatres were an important part of Roman society and in Jerash were three theatres, with the largest and best conserved being the South Theatre, which we toured. I've got some good footage using my camcorder.

In 2007, Petra was named one of the Seven Wonders of the World, and is known for its rock cut architecture. It was constructed around 100 B.C. as the capital city of the Nabataeans. Petra is Jordan's most visited tourism attraction.

Our tour group walked down a road (at least a 40-45 minute walk) into a canyon, which took us into a steep-walled and narrow gorge called the Siq, where at the end of the Siq is Petra's most famous ruin, Al Khazneh, popularly known as The Treasury, hewned into the sandstone cliffs. It's generally believed to be a temple or royal tomb cut into to rock. It was an awesome sight. In the last scenes of the Indiana Jones and the Last Crusade movie, The Treasury is the secret temple where they find the last Crusader guarding the Holy Grail. We rode camels and I took plenty of camcorder footage.

In **Deuteronomy 34: 1-4**, *it is written, [1] And Moses went up from the plains of Moab unto the mountain of Nebo, to the top of Pisgah[a], that is over against Jericho. And the LORD showed him all the land of Gilead, unto Dan, [2] And all Naphtali, and the land* *of Ephraim, and Manasseh, and all the land of Judah, unto the utmost sea, ³ And the south, and the plain of the valley of Jericho, the city of palm trees, unto Zoar. ⁴ And the LORD said unto him, This is the land which I sware unto Abraham, unto Isaac, and unto Jacob, saying, I will give it unto thy seed: I have caused thee to see it with thine eyes, but thou shalt not go over thither.³*

We arrived at Mt. Nebo the 2ⁿᵈ morning of our stay in Jordan. Mt. Nebo is one of the most important Christian sites in Jordan. We visited a church whose history dates back to 2ⁿᵈ half of the fourth century A.D. We could see different mosaic covered floors of the church, representing several periods of the church's history.

Most exciting however, was to look from the summit of Mt. Nebo over into The Holy Land. We could see the city of Jericho directly across from us and to the north, the valley of the Jordan River. Looking south you could see the Jordan River flowing into the Dead Sea.

In **Joshua 1:1-3**, it is written, ¹ Now after the death of Moses the servant of the LORD it came to pass, that the LORD spake unto Joshua the son of Nun, Moses' minister, saying, ² Moses my servant is dead; now therefore arise, go over this Jordan, thou, and all this people, unto the land which I do give to them, *even* to the children of Israel. ³ Every place that the sole of your

---

³*The Holy Bible : King James Version.* 1995 . Logos Research Systems, Inc.: Oak Harbor, WA

foot shall tread upon, that have I given unto you, as I said unto Moses.[4]

From Mt. Nebo we crossed over into Israel at the Allenby Bridge crossing, and we ourselves crossed over in the Promised Land.

Israel

Crossing over the Allenby Bridge into Israel required all 24 of our tour group to show our passports and visas at the border crossing checkpoint. There were Jordanian armed guards with large caliber machine guns on the Jordanian side of the bridge, and armed Israeli guards, with similar large caliber machine guns on the Israeli side of the bridge. It was a stark reminder of the tension in that area of the world. Once cleared, we'd go to be baptized in the Jordan River, then we'd drive several hours in our tour bus on our way to the City of Tiberias, located on the west side of the Sea of Galilee. This is where our tour of Israel would begin.

In reviewing the itinerary of the Holy Land tour, it seemed to me that our tour would visit many of the places mentioned in the book of Matthew, and so it was. I will briefly note some of the many places we toured in Israel.

---

[4]*The Holy Bible : King James Version.* 1995 . Logos Research Systems, Inc.: Oak Harbor, WA

Water Baptized - Our first stop in Israel was being baptized in the Jordan River. Bertha & I have some great photos taken by us and of us.

Tiberius & The Sea of Galilee – We took a boat and went out onto the Sea of Galilee, where Pastor Gary gave a sermon. Later that evening I mentioned to Pastor Gary that I felt something different in my spirit that I never felt before. He said that my human spirit was at home, that's why I felt differently.

Capernaum – This is place where Jesus gave the Sermon on the Mount.

Megiddo – We went up to Mt. Megiddo, the hill over looking the valley, identified in the bible, as the site of the final battle between good and evil at the end of time, known as Armageddon.

Jerusalem – It was extremely exciting seeing Jerusalem from the tour bus. The first thing I noticed was the Dome of the Rock. We stopped at a high vantage point overlooking the city and the wall around the Old City of Jerusalem. In 1000 BC, King David established Jerusalem as the capital of the Jewish nation and Solomon his son would later build the first temple in the city. We stayed at The Olive Tree Hotel in Jerusalem, which was under armed guard 24 hours per day. On our first full day, we toured the Western Wall, known as the Wailing Wall, and we walked past the Dome of the Rock. We would come back to visit the city a couple of more times.

Bethlehem – The town of Jesus' birth. We toured the Church of the Nativity, where it is said that the manger was in a cave beneath the church. We viewed an area beneath the church said to be where Jesus was born. Bethlehem is in the Palestinian controlled area of Israel so we had to go through another security checkpoint to get to and from Bethlehem.

Mount of Olives - This hill has a significant location in biblical events and prophesied events of the last days. Here, Jesus will return in the last days. In ***Zechariah 14: 4-5***, it is written, [4] *And his feet shall stand in that day upon the mount of Olives, which is before Jerusalem on the east, and the mount of Olives shall cleave in the midst thereof toward the east and toward the west, and there shall be a very great valley; and half of the mountain shall remove toward the north, and half of it toward the south.* [5] *And ye shall flee to the valley of the mountains[a]; for the valley of the mountains shall reach unto Azal: yea, ye shall flee, like as ye fled from before the earthquake in the days of Uzziah king of Judah: and the LORD my God shall come, and all the saints with thee.*[5]

Our tour group stood on the Mount of Olives and viewed the Eastern Gate to the City of Jerusalem, where Jesus made his

---

a the mountains: or, my mountains

[5]*The Holy Bible: King James Version.* 1995. Logos Research Systems, Inc.: Oak Harbor, WA

triumphal entry on Palm Sunday.

Garden of Gethsemane – We walked around the Garden of Gethsemane taking in the significance of the garden, in that this was the place Judas came to betray Jesus. Botanists claim that some of the olive trees in the garden are over 3,000 years, meaning that some of the trees were here long before and during Jesus' time in the garden. I touched many of the trees as I prayed in the spirit.

Palace of Caiaphas – We toured the site of the Palace of Caiaphas. Caiaphas was the High Priest in Jerusalem at the time of Jesus' arrest and crucifixion. Outside of the palace is where Peter denied Jesus three times.

Via Dolorosa - This is the traditional pathway that Jesus traveled to Calvary or Golgotha, the English language/Western Christian names given the site of the crucifixion. We walked that path, which was now filled with merchants. When we reached Calvary/Golgotha, Pastor Gary preached a sermon on the location as it was noted in the various gospels. If you looked at the rock formation on the hill, you could actually see what looked like a face or skull, which supports the Greek translation of Golgotha.

Garden Tomb – We visited the Garden Tomb where tradition has it that Jesus was buried. Bertha and I went in the tomb separately so one of us could take camcorder footage of the other going in and coming out of the tomb. This was exhilarating because Jesus was resurrected and with his resurrection we rose together with him. This was another **WOW** moment for me! I believe that if you are a born-again-believer, once you go to Israel, your life will never be the same. I believe you will have seen and experienced too much to be the same person that you were before you went to Israel.

With our stay ending in Jerusalem, we headed back to Amman, Jordan for our return flight to the United States of America.

I need to mention that 2005 was the best year Bertha and I would experience in the residential real estate market. Our real estate business allowed us the time and generated the income to travel extensively and we cheerfully gave our tithes and offerings.

First Holy Spirit Unctions

In June 1995, I received two unctions from the Holy Spirit. An unction can be described as a thought from the Holy Spirit. The only way I can describe how I knew it came from the Holy Spirit, is that I felt it in *my spirit. (Note: You've heard the expression, "I had a gut feeling". This statement is from someone who is not a spirit-filled believer. A spirit–filled believer knows that "gut-feeling" is your human spirit talking to you).* The first unction I wrote down was, "***When a God-given opportunity, meets a Holy Spirit prepared person, God-given success is***

the result". I had been thinking about the world's definition of success, which is, "when preparedness meets opportunity, success result" (something like that), when I received the unction.

When I received this unction, I wrote it down and dated it. The more I thought on the unction, I ended up with this statement, ***"When a Prepared Spirit-filled Believer Meets a God-given Opportunity, the God-kind of Success Results."*** This was now my definition of success.

The second unction came a few days later and it was, ***"We have no control over when a God-given opportunity will present itself, but we do control being spiritually prepared".***

It would be a little over two years before these two statements would take root and begin to bear fruit in my life. I will return to the impact of unctions in my life a little later in this writing.

For a 2005 Christmas present, Bertha bought me Germaine Copeland's *"Prayers That Avail Much"* book. This book is a joy to read and has prayers of praise to God, Jesus, and the Holy Spirit, and for whatever situations the world may bring you, your family, friends, colleagues, and acquaintances. I have used with permission from Germaine Copland's publisher, three references from the Chapter entitled, "Adoration: Hallowed Be Thy Name", in a prayer that I pray, and am publishing here. The name of my prayer is, "Adoration Prayer".

Adoration Prayer

Heavenly Father, I praise your name.

Father, I give you praise, I give you glory, I give you honor. I give you adoration,

I give you thanksgiving.

Father, I worship you and I adore you because I know who you are.

You are **Jehovah-Jireh**, the One who sees my needs and provides for them. Hallowed be Thy Name!

You are **El-Shaddai,** the God Almighty of blessings. You are the Breasty One Who nourishes and supplies. You are all-bountiful and you are all-sufficient. Hallowed be Thy Name!

You are **Jehovah-Shalom**. You are my Peace. The peace that transcends all understanding. Hallowed be Thy Name!

Father, I know your 12 redemptive names. I know your character. And because I know you, I have access to you.

Thank you Father, In Jesus Name!

The greatest thing in the life we live is **salvation**! With salvation comes God's character. However, if you don't know God's character, you will miss out on what you have access to.

CHAPTER 13
SPIRITUAL GROWTH 2007

Alaska

To celebrate our 11th wedding anniversary, Bertha & I decided to go on a cruise to Alaska. I probably booked the cruise in January 2006, paid with cash. Our travel itinerary, handled by Carnival Cruise Lines, would fly us out of the Baltimore/Washington International Airport (BWI), to Dallas, TX, to Vancouver, British Columbia., where we would board the Carnival Spirit and sail out at 5:30PM, Pacific Standard Time.

We arrived at BWI in plenty of time and went to the ticket counter, where we encountered a major problem. The FAA requires a minimum amount of minutes between connecting flights, in this case between the time we landed in Dallas, TX and getting on a plane to Vancouver. The time was something like 47 minutes that was required under FAA guidelines and the flight that Carnival had booked was 43 minutes between connecting flights. The ticket counter person at BWI said we could fly to Dallas, but we could not get the connecting flight to Vancouver. We initially thought there had to be a way around this minor problem, but after going through two levels of management, it sunk in that we were not able to get on the flight from Dallas to Vancouver. Panic set in. Bertha asked me if I had heard in my spirit that we were not going on our cruise. I said I had not heard that. We were going on our cruise and Bertha and I began praying in the spirit.

Carnival had given us a number to call in case of an emergency, which we called. It was truly a blessing that I had carried along our cell phone adapter, which allowed us to plug the cell phone adapter into an electrical outlet and not have to worry about our battery running out. Bertha talked with Carnival for close to two hours, being on hold, most of the time. While she was on hold, we both continued to pray in the spirit.

Carnival began working to get us on a flight out of BWI to Vancouver. Their initial plan called for our being booked on another flight out of BWI, which caused us to have to move very quickly to another terminal at BWI. We grabbed a baggage person with a baggage cart and we ran for what seemed like 15 to 20 minutes to the next terminal, only to find out that the plane had just left. This news caused Bertha to cry uncontrollably. I felt calm in my spirit, and I explained our situation to ticket counter person, who called and spoke to

Carnival about our missing the flight that they had set up.

Carnival said they would call back the ticket counter person in a few minutes. I told Bertha that everything was going to work out and I prayed in the spirit again. A few minutes later, Carnival called back and said we had to get to Reagan National Airport in Washington, DC to catch a flight to Toronto, Canada, and from there a flight to Vancouver. I forget which airline they said go to, but we went outside the terminal, hailed a cab, and off to Reagan National Airport we went. The cab driver was sympathetic to our problem and not a single vehicle passed us on the way to Reagan National. Most of the way going to Reagan, I was on the phone talking to Carnival. Thank God for the battery charging adapter. They instructed me to call them once I reach Reagan National.

Once we got to Reagan National, where the ticket counter person was expecting us, Carnival said to call them as we were boarding the flight to Toronto, which I did. They further instructed me that once we reached the gate in Toronto getting ready to board the flight to Vancouver, to call them, which I did. Next, I was told once we got to the Vancouver Airport, go to Baggage Claims and look for the Carnival Shuttle to the Cruise Ship pier, which we did. We were told exactly what documents to have in-hand so as to expedite our boarding the cruise ship at the pier.

We're finally on the shuttle to the Cruise Ship pier, but we're on the eastern side of the city, and have to go to the western side of the city, and its rush hour! That was bad enough, but our driver, who was from India, seemed like he was taking his time, describing many of the places along the way, as it was getting close to 5:30PM Pacific Standard Time, the cruise ship departing time. Bertha and I continued to pray in the spirit.

We finally get to the Carnival Cruise Ship pier and there are **no people there**, except for three Carnival Cruise Ship personnel **waiting for us**. As we walked across the gangway to the ship, the ship was conducting lifeboat drills, and many, many people clapped for us. We were the **last people aboard** the Carnival Spirit and within 15 minutes, the ship was leaving the pier. A couple of times aboard ship, people stopped us and asked us if we were that couple who barely made it aboard ship. We told them yes we were, by the grace of God.

Our cruise to Alaska would turn out to be our most exciting and adventurous cruise that we've ever taken. On the second day of our cruise, we enjoyed a magnificent day at sea cruising the Inside Passage. We stopped at Ketchikan, Juneau, the capital of Alaska, Skagway, Sitka, and we cruised through Price William Sound, and College Fjord. At each stop we went on excursions seeing humpback whales, sea otters, bears, and so many eagles. We cruised near magnificent glaciers, witnessed glacier walls falling into the sea, and the terrain of Alaska was breathtaking. We left the cruise ship in Whittier, Alaska, and traveled by bus to Anchorage, where we boarded our non-stop flight to Baltimore/Washington International Airport.

We have lots of great photos and camcorder footage. Bertha and I thanked God for our 11 years of marriage and we particularly thanked him for **His favor** that we received getting to the cruise ship. Bertha and I believe that *praying in the spirit* activated God's favor on our behalf.

Keep Her Alive Until I Get There

On Monday afternoon, October 16, 2006, Bertha received a phone call from Arlington Hospital in Dallas, TX. Felicia, Bertha's only daughter, had been brought in to the ER unresponsive and on life support. They told us some decisions had to be made. They said that Felicia had suffered a brain bleed or stroke. They said that 9 out of 10 patients with her condition don't survive. Bertha called Felicia's father and told him the situation. Bertha and Felicia's father spoke with the doctor on a three-way phone connection. The prognosis was very bad and the decision that had to be made at this time was to remove her from life support or keep her alive until someone could get to the hospital. The nursed asked if Felicia's organs could be donated. That's how sure the hospital staff was that Felicia was not going to make it. Felicia's father would allow her to be removed from life support, but Bertha told the doctor, "keep her alive until I get there"! Bertha and I prayed about what to do next. Bertha decided we would go to bed and make our decision when we got up around 4AM for our morning prayer.

The next morning, after our prayer time, we decided that

Bertha would go to Dallas and I'd stay home and keep our business going. Bertha had a first cousin, Essie, that lived 20 miles south of Dallas and upon hearing the news about Felicia, told Bertha that she could stay with her for as long as necessary and would give Bertha a car to drive. I booked her a flight that morning and put her on a plane that afternoon.

This would be only the 2nd time in our 11 years of marriage that Bertha had ever been away from me. The first time occurred in 2003 when she went to Los Angeles for 4 days because of her sister's death. On Thursday, I went to Victory for our prayer service night and I got up and told the congregation our situation with Felicia and the whole church lifted her up in prayer.

Felicia was in a coma and still required a breathing apparatus. Bertha is a prayer warrior and she knew that she was in spiritual warfare, such that she went and bought camouflage combat fatigues and shoes. It didn't matter to her that this type of dress was in Vogue, she was at war to bring her daughter back from the dead. She would get to the hospital at 9AM and stay to 5 or 6PM everyday. She would pray and read the bible to Felicia. She would talk to her and rub her hands and arms and feet. Kiss her forehead and cheeks. A friend of the family, Jackie, who lived in Dallas, who hadn't seen Bertha in many years, also came to the hospital and spent time with Bertha and Felicia. Many times Jackie would buy Bertha lunch in the hospital cafeteria. Many other family members also stopped by to see Felicia.

Then, one day as Bertha was praying by Felicia's bedside, Bertha told Felicia to move her feet, and praise God, Felicia's foot moved. This happened 7 or 8 days after Bertha arrived at the hospital. Felicia was coming back!

I went to Dallas three weeks after Bertha left and stayed for 4 days. I went back for Thanksgiving and Felicia was able to sit in her wheelchair and could maneuver herself around.

On December 7th, Felicia left the hospital under her own power and on December 9th, she flew back to Delaware with Bertha to live with us for about 7 months. I can still remember when she came to Victory with us that first Sunday. She was a walking miracle and the congregation recognized and applauded her. Many in the church saw the manifestation of their prayers. It was a joyous day.

In our relationship with Felicia as she lived with us, she became a constant in our prayer life. The stroke left her partially paralyzed on our right side and she would have a permanent trac tube in her throat. Bertha and I were believing for a healing miracle in her life. Bertha and I said, and continue to say, that we have a front row seat to this miracle that will take place. However, Felicia's lifestyle and the choices that she makes would impact the probability of her miracle ever happening. The first and most important thing that Felicia had to do was to respect her mother, which in many cases she did not, even after all that Bertha had done and was continuing to do for her. The bible clearly says in **Exodus 20:12, "Honour**

thy father and thy mother: that thy days may be long ...".
This lack of honour was a concern to Bertha and me. I said to
Felicia that God was going to get his Glory through her, with or
without her cooperation. Because of Felicia's attitude and her
physical situation, the Holy Spirit brought the following prayer
to my spirit concerning her. After a while, I realized that this
prayer applies to everyone, even children and young adults. So,
in the blank name field of this prayer, insert whoever's name
you want. The prayer is entitled, "**Doer and Hearer Prayer**".

Doer and Hearer Prayer

For Adults

Father, we thank you that ________ would come to **know** and
understand and **experience** your *Word* more **perfectly,** so
that he/she would be a **doer** of your Word and not a **hearer**
only *(James 1:22)*. We pray that his/her **experiences** will be
part of their **testimony** and that they will **serve** you.

For Teenagers and Children

Father, we thank you that ________ would come to **know** and
understand and **experience** your *Word* at an **early age** so
that he/she would be a **doer** of your Word and not a **hearer**
only. We pray that his/her **experiences** will be part of their
testimony and that they will **serve** you.

Spiritual Growth 2007

Dorothy Toulson Earl

Dorothy Toulson Earl was my mother and Bertha's best friend on the East coast. One of the greatest things I remember about Mom was the day we talked about how she always prayed for me and sometimes would cry herself to sleep because of my drinking and associated behavior. Dad had gone home to be with the Lord for a few years now. As I usually would, I'd stop by and see Mom sometimes in the morning on my way to work or on my way home. This particular day, I was telling Mom about how happy I was about my marriage, Gebrette being back in my life and how her siblings accepted and loved her, the real estate business, Victory Christian Fellowship, which Mom started attending periodically, and other good things that were happening in my life. Bertha and I were traveling, going on cruises and life was generally very good. That's when she told me about all the nights, throughout the years, of her prayers and tears. She was so happy to see that I had turned out alright, and she thanked Bertha in part for that. She appreciated the fact that I and Bertha were here to take care of her.

The only time she had any concern was when Bertha and I traveled. She knew that Demetria was only 30 minutes away if she needed her, and George, Jr. could be there in 90 minutes if she needed him.

On Thursday, May 10th, I again stopped by to see Mom and check up on her. Bertha and I would be flying out the next day to Los Angeles for our Mexican Rivera Cruise, leaving San Diego on Sunday, celebrating our 12th wedding anniversary. We sat down at the kitchen table and for about an hour we just talked. I got up from the table and stood for another 20-30 minutes talking, while standing in the doorway from the dining room to the kitchen. I kissed her on the forehead, told her I loved her, and said I'd see her when we got back. I told her I'd call her when I got to Los Angeles.

The next morning the shuttle came to pick us up about 4AM to take us to the Philadelphia International Airport. I asked the driver to stop by Mom's house so I could leave her a Mother's day present, since Sunday would be Mother's Day. We arrived at LAX where Joyce and Sam picked us up, and took us to their home. Bertha and I were planning to attend an Urban Bankers Association (UBA) function that evening with our friend Betty, who was instrumental in Bertha and I meeting back in 1994. Betty was gracious enough to allow us to stay in her hotel suite and be her guest at the UBA function. After the function, Bertha and I went back to the hotel suite and planned on getting a good night sleep. We had a busy day planned for Saturday, and we needed to re-pack for our Mexican Rivera cruise.

At 4:36AM (PST) Saturday morning, my cell phone rang and it was my daughter Demetria on the phone. She and my ex-wife were at Mom's house and they were on their way to the hospital. Mom had called Demetria complaining of a very bad headache. I didn't think much of it except I was glad that

Demetria and my ex-wife were there for Mom. I went back to sleep immediately.

Two hours later, my cell phone rang again, and this time it was my daughter Angie, who is a medical doctor. She was crying and she told me that Mom had suffered a massive stroke and she didn't have long to live. Angie said she had spoken to the neurologist and there was nothing that could be done to reverse the diagnosis. Angie said I had two choices. They could keep her alive until I got back, or they could make sure she was in no pain and let her pass when it was her time. I told Angie to tell the doctors to make sure Mom was in no pain and I would get home as soon as possible. I then called Betty and she came to the hotel to get Bertha and me and took us back to Joyce's house. Shortly after arriving at Joyce's house, the neurologist called me and informed me personally about Mom's situation, which broke me down. He repeated the two options Angie mentioned and I again said make sure she was in no pain and let pass when it was her time. I asked to speak to Angie, and she told me that all five of the grandchildren were at Mom's bedside. I told her that I was on my way to LAX and once I had arranged my flight back, I'd call her and let her know what time I'd arrive in Philadelphia.

When we arrived at LAX, I checked our luggage at the curb while Bertha went to the ticket counter. There was a line of people, but Bertha, in tears, went right to the ticket person, excused herself and she we had to get back to Philadelphia ASAP. The ticket counter person was very kind and we got booked on the next flight out to Philadelphia, by way of Atlanta.

I called Angie, and told her the time I'd be arriving in Atlanta and what time I'd be in Philadelphia. Once I got to Atlanta, I would talk to George, who would be picking me up in Philadelphia. I got to Atlanta and called George, who was crying, and he told me that Mom had passed away about two hours ago.

At 85, Mom had lived a very good life. She was able to know her five grandchildren loved her deeply, all five had college degrees, two of which were doctors - an OB/GYN and an orthopedic surgeon. She had seen six of her seven great grandchildren. She knew her son was very happy and doing well in his life. The funeral arrangements went very smoothly. Many family members contributed time, money and effort. We had a wonderful going home ceremony.

Health and Marriage Prayer

Soon after Mom's death, I began to pray the following prayer each and every morning. I knew Mom's father, my grandfather, who we called Pop, had also died of a stroke, so my passing away from a stroke crossed my mind.

Health and Marriage Prayer

*Father, my wife and I thank you for **this** day.*

I thank you for my health and for my strength. I thank you for renewing my mind and my body.

I thank you that I am healed from the top of my head, to the soles of my feet.

I thank you that there are no stroke symptoms, there are no HIV, there are no AIDS, there are no cancerous cells in my body.

*I thank you that I have a very strong heart and that each and every cell is operating as **You** designed it.*

———————————————————

Father, I thank you for my wife. I thank you for her love. I thank you for her health and for her strength.

I thank you for renewing her mind and her body.

I thank you that she is healed from the top of her head to the soles of her feet.

I thank you that there are no stroke symptoms, there are no HIV, there are no AIDS, there are no cancerous cells in her body.

*I thank you that she has a very strong heart and that each and every cell is operating as **You** designed it.*

Father, I thank you for our marriage and our sweet and tender love making, and I believe it will continue for many, many, many, many, many, many, many more years in the Name of Jesus.

This prayer is important to me for the three most important things is my life.

1) My health and my strength
2) Bertha's health and her strength
3) Our marriage

For if any one of these three things were not as they should be, I'd have a very serious problem. Bertha is in total agreement with me on these three things as to their importance in her life.

I have previously mentioned that most of the time Bertha and I pray together each morning. I also noted that we read a chapter of Proverb for whatever day of the month it is. On the 30th or 31st of every month, I always read **Proverbs 31** from the *Amplified Bible* to Bertha. I've been reading this to her since 2007. This chapter, beginning in verse 10, talks about a virtuous woman, and I read this to my wife with *vigor* each month. **She is my Proverbs 31 woman!** Men, I strongly encourage you to read this chapter *(from the Amplified Bible)* to your wife each month, even if she's not quite there yet. I know that it will encourage her to be all that God's Word says she is. Wash her with the water of the Word and she will love you just a little bit more.

In 2007, we added another set of scriptures from the *Amplified Bible* that we read to one another to add further enrichment to our Morning Prayer and praise time. In the books of Ephesians and Colossians, the Apostle Paul writes to the new Christians at these churches, praying for them. In reading these scriptures, some of them are certainly appropriate for me to read to Bertha and for Bertha to read to me. So, what Bertha and I do is to read the below scriptures to one another. There are three sets of scriptures. I may read all three sets to Bertha or she may read all three sets to me. Or, I may read one set and she reads the other set. Or, we may read every other scripture to each other in a given set. It really all depends on how the Spirit moves us. In any case, we are washing each other with the Word of God. We don't read these scriptures everyday, maybe once or twice a week to each other.

Prayers for Each Other

Ephesians 1: 15-23

15 For this reason **George/Bertha**, because I have heard of your faith in the Lord Jesus and your love toward all the saints (the people of God),

16 I do not cease to give thanks for you, making mention of you in my prayers.

17 [For I always pray to] the God of our Lord Jesus Christ, the Father of glory, that He may grant you **George/Bertha** a spirit of wisdom and revelation [of insight into mysteries and secrets] in the [deep and intimate] knowledge of Him,

18 By having the eyes of your heart flooded with light, so that you **George/Bertha** can know *and* understand the hope to which He has called you, and how rich is His glorious inheritance in the saints (His set-apart ones),

19 And [so that you **George/Bertha** can know and understand] what is the immeasurable *and* unlimited *and* surpassing greatness of His power in *and* for us who believe, as demonstrated in the working of His mighty strength,

20 Which He exerted in Christ when He raised Him from the dead and seated Him at His [own] right hand in the heavenly [places],

21 Far above all rule and authority and power and dominion and every name that is named [above every title that

can be conferred], not only in this age *and* in this world, but also in the age *and* the world which are to come.

22 And He has put all things under His feet and has appointed Him the universal and supreme Head of the church [a headship exercised throughout the church], [Ps. 8:6.]

23 Which is His body, the fullness of Him Who fills all in all [for in that body lives the full measure of Him Who makes everything complete, and Who fills everything everywhere with Himself].[6]

Ephesians 3: 14-21

14 For this reason **George/Bertha** [seeing the greatness of this plan by which you are built together in Christ], I bow my knees before the Father *of our Lord Jesus Christ,*

15 For Whom every family in heaven and on earth is named [that Father from Whom all fatherhood takes its title and derives its name].

16 May He grant you **George/Bertha** out of the rich treasury of His glory to be strengthened *and* reinforced with mighty power in the inner man by the [Holy] Spirit [Himself indwelling your innermost being and personality].

---

[6]*The amplified Bible, containing the amplified Old Testament and the amplified New Testament.* 1987 . The Lockman Foundation: La Habra, CA

17 May Christ through your faith **George/Bertha** [actually] dwell (settle down, abide, make His permanent home) in your hearts! May you **George/Bertha** be rooted deep in love *and* founded securely on love,

18 That you **George/Bertha** may have the power *and* be strong to apprehend *and* grasp with all the saints [God's devoted people, the experience of that love] what is the breadth and length and height and depth [of it];

19 [That you **George/Bertha** may really come] to know [practically, through experience for yourself] the love of Christ, which far surpasses mere knowledge [without experience]; that you **George/Bertha** may be filled [through all your being] unto all the fullness of God [may have the richest measure of the divine Presence, and you George/Bertha become a body wholly filled and flooded with God Himself]!

20 Now to Him Who, by (in consequence of) the [action of His] power that is at work within you **George/Bertha**, is able to [carry out His purpose and] do superabundantly, far over *and* above all that you **George/Bertha** [dare] ask or think [infinitely beyond your highest prayers, desires, thoughts, hopes, or dreams]—

21 To Him be glory in the church and in Christ Jesus throughout all generations forever and ever. Amen (so be it).[7]

---

[7]*The amplified Bible, containing the amplified Old Testament and the amplified New Testament.* 1987 . The Lockman Foundation: La Habra, CA

Colossians 1: 9-23

9 For this reason **George/Bertha** we also, from the day we heard of it, have not ceased to pray *and* make [special] request for you, [asking] that you **George/Bertha** may be filled with the full (deep and clear) knowledge of His will in all spiritual wisdom [in comprehensive insight into the ways and purposes of God] and in understanding *and* discernment of spiritual things—

10 That you **George/Bertha** may walk (live and conduct yourselves) in a manner worthy of the Lord, fully pleasing to Him *and* desiring to please Him in all things, bearing fruit in every good work and steadily growing *and* increasing in *and* by the knowledge of God [with fuller, deeper, and clearer insight, acquaintance, and recognition].

11 [We pray] that you **George/Bertha** may be invigorated *and* strengthened with all power according to the might of His glory, [to exercise] every kind of endurance and patience (perseverance and forbearance) with joy,

12 Giving thanks to the Father, Who has qualified *and* made you **George/Bertha** fit to share the portion which is the inheritance of the saints (God's holy people) in the Light.

13 [The Father] has delivered *and* drawn us to Himself out of the control *and* the dominion of darkness and has transferred you **George/Bertha** into the kingdom of the Son of His love,

14 In Whom we have our redemption *through His blood,* [which means] the forgiveness of our sins.

15 [Now] He is the exact likeness of the unseen God [the visible representation of the invisible]; He is the Firstborn of all creation.

16 For it was in Him that all things were created, in heaven and on earth, things seen and things unseen, whether thrones, dominions, rulers, or authorities; all things were created *and* exist through Him [by His service, intervention] and in *and* for Him.

17 And He Himself existed before all things, and in Him all things consist (cohere, are held together). [Prov. 8:22-31.]

18 He also is the Head of [His] body, the church; seeing He is the Beginning, the Firstborn from among the dead, so that He alone in everything *and* in every respect might occupy the chief place [stand first and be preeminent].

19 For it has pleased [the Father] that all the divine fullness (the sum total of the divine perfection, powers, and attributes) should dwell in Him permanently.

20 And God purposed that through (by the service, the intervention of) Him [the Son] all things should be completely reconciled back to Himself, whether on earth or in heaven, as through Him, [the Father] made peace by means of the blood of His cross.

21 And although you **George/Bertha** at one time were estranged *and* alienated from Him and were of hostile attitude of mind in your wicked activities,

22 Yet now has [Christ, the Messiah] reconciled [you to God] in the body of His flesh through death, in order to present

you holy and faultless and irreproachable in His [the Father's] presence.[8]

<hr>

[8]*The amplified Bible, containing the amplified Old Testament and the amplified New Testament.* 1987 . The Lockman Foundation: La Habra, CA

CHAPTER 14
TRAPS OF THE OFFENDED

In late fall of 2007, the leaders of the Marriage Fellowship asked us to speak at our First Friday event. Bertha read a **powerful** piece she had just written and she led a discussion on her piece, which is included here. It is entitled, **"Traps of the Offended"**.

Traps of the Offended

Offense is defined as anger, resentment, hurt or displeasure. Spiritually, an offense on the born again believer can cause her/him to become entrapped by bitterness; Out of the place of security in Christ. Out of the "Secret Place of The Most High", as Psalms 91 describes, into the flesh where the enemy has control. Even though the Word tells us to "walk in the spirit" and not fulfill the lust of the flesh, when we are offended, the hurt, anger and resentment traps the believer and jeopardizes his standing with The Lord, His fellowman and himself/herself, as well.

As a wife, mother, sister, and church member, there have been many occasions to be offended. Women are considered "emotional"; Wives the weaker sex. According to the Word, husbands are alerted in this regard, 1 Peter 3:7, "Likewise You Husbands…". In other words, women are more susceptible to being offended. Once the offense has happened, if not dealt with according to God's Word, a root of bitterness which, if not bound and cast out, is the result. Eventually, "a stronghold" of the enemy can be constructed. Like a New York Ticker Tape, every time you think of the hurt, it is more difficult than the previous time to get rid of it. It goes around and around; you keep thinking about it over and over and over again. In particular, when you sit down to eat a meal, you will find that thought, that infraction, that hurt, coming back to you over and over again! It is little wonder why people eat too much or too little or eat or drink the wrong things. The Word tells us to stop the hurt or insult at the onset – the thought! (Phil 4:8). Heb 12:15 says, see that no root of bitterness spring up in you, trouble you and thereby defile you.

In the world there was a popular recording, "It's a thin line between love and hate". There was even a movie made with that title. What was conveyed is between love mates. You can be in strong passionate love one minute, and then the next minute you are throwing hot grits, or burning up some one's clothing, or even in a place where one partner either kills another or is as passionately angry as he/she was in love. That kind of love is worldly, not at all Godly.

As a wife, you may have been ignored, or talked to sharply by your husband. What about after making passionate love the night before, you find yourself in a disagreement, and you feel like your husband was totally different from that night? You feel hurt and unappreciated, betrayed and maybe even misused. You feel as though he was not the same man as the one in your marriage bed. Your feelings are hurt. I remember George's former pastor saying, "Brother George, if "Bert" ever misbehaves as your wife, she is still your sister in Christ and must be treated as such". 1 Cor 13 tells you what love really is. Love is not a feeling – It is a commitment! Matt 22:40 says on the law of love hang all other commandments. Love your neighbor as yourself. When you exercise love, the love of God, there is no co-existence with hate. Love covers a multitude of faults and sins. In love, there is no competition or conflict. You relinquish your position (which in the natural you may be entitled to) for the other person. There are no harsh words. My girlfriend gave me good advice when she said, "Bertha, you can always say more later."

You don't try to crush another person with your words. JUST GOTTA GET IT OUT.

It was in the early 1980's when a young lady who obviously had seen my outward expressions to the events of some wrongdoing in a Church I had recently come to join, came up to me and said, "Bertha, offenses are a trap". That's all she said. She looked me straight in the eye on a Sunday and said again,

"Bertha, offenses are a trap!"

Befuddled and disoriented as to how she knew my thoughts, I pondered my inward and outward appearances and concluded this as a "Word of Knowledge", "A Word of Wisdom" or "Discerning of Spirits". It was to my advantage, that the Lord would make me aware of some flaws in my own life which could cause my demise. For it was in that moment and probably many more, I judged this ministry. God is the Judge, and admonished me to keep my eyes on Him and not the vessels he had chosen for that ministry.

What happened to me, because of the Trap of Offense, would take me on a long journey which would last twelve years, day in and day out trying to understand someone else's wrongdoing in my own eyesight. My entire life, ministry and career would careen in a downward spiral. In hurt and despair I prayed and cried, and wondered why God was allowing such abuse to happen in this church, not only to me, but to the hundreds and hundreds of other members, family and friends.

The Word of God tells us in Matt 7:1, "Judge not that ye be not judged". I knew that, but this is so obvious, Lord! Then I heard, "Touch not my anointed (1 Ch 6:22) and do my prophets no harm". He said His gifts were without repentance. So long as the pastors stood before us, people were saved, delivered and set free. God had anointed them, just like He did Saul. I spent 12 years being injured day in and day out looking at all the maneuvers and strategies of the people. Leaving the church was not an option. I had to learn to survive my personal hurts, which drove me to God and the Holy Spirit. I found out I was there as an intercessor, which was my gift and anointing from God. So, I interceded. I had been trained in earlier years as a "gap warrior" based on Ezek 22:30, "I sought for a man among them, that should make up the hedge and stand in the gap before me for the Land". So, I prayed without ceasing.

At that point, I knew why I had left a thriving ministry where everyone was flourishing and had come to this small, but vibrant ministry where everyone and everything was in my face. I could see the Pastors on their good days and their bad days. I could see how the church was growing by the multitude of salvations and deliverances. I could also see the "wounded soldiers". I needed to "Stand In The Gap"! I would dream of the pastors over and over again, and end up praying hours at a time. I told the pastors my dreams. And they would say, "Keep on praying Bertha".

There were Prayer Warriors in that church who thought it nothing to stay up all night praying in order to touch the heart of God and the life of the believer. We would come to the church at 5:00 in the morning even though sometime the pastors were not there to let us in. In the cold and dark, the Prayer Warriors would stand outside and travail, laying their hands on the fence. It was shocking to hear prophecies coming through the pastors which uncovered hidden sins and exposed Satan in an unprecedented way. Gang members turned in their head rags. Drug dealers brought their dope and guns in a display of true repentance. Prostitutes fell on the altar and became ushers and teachers.

The dichotomy, was now I see the fleshly side of God's chosen vessels. How was I going to handle that? Was I going to run to my old church 40 miles away from my new home? Was I going to seek another church close by? Was I going to murmur and complain and bring God's judgment on myself? What am I going to do? I decided to pray and watch God do what He does in me, the pastors, and the parishioners.

This morning, thinking on some current events here at Victory, I began to question some things. Actually, I was using my mind to make sense of them. – JUDGING! The Holy Spirit brought to my mind again, "Bertha, offenses are a trap"! I thought about how only God knows the hearts and intents of man (1 Sam 16:7). I looked on the outside appearance. He reminded me of God's sovereignty. I heard in my spirit, how can you see the speck in your brother's eye, with that plank in yours (Matt 7:3-5)?

As usually the oldest child at home out of a clan of 10, I was in charge of exacting out justice on my siblings based on listening to each side. I then reported to my parents in a detailed manner. They took care of the punishments based on my copious notes. When my parents chose a different conclusion than I surmised, I would voice my opinion (in a manner provided for only on Saturday Nights, where we all got to talk). Outside of those meetings, I got slapped in the mouth. When my parents argued, I was the referee and used the Bible as my authority. They didn't like that. They got divorced anyway.

As a high school student and later college student, I always asked questions. When I came to be a student of the Bible, I did the same thing. As a leader in Christian circles, I related to Moses and what a rough time he had with the Children of Israel. Why didn't he get to go into the Promised Land? I thought about the brother of the Prodigal Son. He was faithful to his father, yet the prodigal got the attention when he finally showed up. I understood the humanity of Martha, Mary's sister. How she always did the work while her sister sat around and enjoyed Jesus. Why is it that David was the apple of God's eye, even though he did so much wrong? Job was doing well until God reminded Satan of how blessed Job was. Then he lost everything - Why? Peter was only trying to let Jesus know how much he loved Him, but Jesus said, "thou art an offense to me". Why did Jacob get away with Esau's blessing? Remember the parable of the ten talents? Why did He take from the one and give to the guy who already had 10?

I don't know about you, but I have thought about these things. What about the person at work who got a promotion, while I worked like a slave and got nothing, but eventually fired? A Trap! Why God? Where is the justice in this? Many times in life, I was hurt and had resentment about things that seemed unfair. I went on a campaign to change them. Who eventually got hurt was me! I don't know why bad things happen to good people.

What I do know is that God is good, all the time. He is all the while working in me both to will and do of His good pleasure (Phil 2:13). I know that God says I know the plans I have for you (Jer. 29:11, to prosper you and give you hope and a future). Why didn't I think about all the times He brought me out of situations I had no business being involved with? Did I remember the time when I was in the wrong place and could have been raped, but I called out the Name of Jesus and the perpetrator freed me? What about when the court judge did not find me in contempt of court, though it really could have been proven the other way? The Lord provided me with a blessed marriage, even though it was my <u>third time!</u> His love toward me said, "You will not be an outcast. I know your heart". When I think about the goodness of the Lord towards me, my soul cries Hallelujah! Thank you God for loving me! He is so faithful to help me raise six children as a single parent. It was God who made provision for me to return to Pepperdine University on a full scholarship, graduate summa cum laude, after the age of 32, while raising my own three children and on welfare.

I didn't mention how He delivered my daughter from a stroke last year when the doctors said, "ten patients have come in this hospital like her and she is the only one going out"! I don't know. The more I think I can figure God out, the more I find out what I don't know about Him, especially when I try to judge some other individual's life. God is Good! His Mercies endure forever! G-R-A-C-E, <u>God's Riches At Christ's Expense</u>.

The outcome of the ministry in the aforementioned church

came to disaster. After some years, the pastors divorced and married other people two more times. They had each been married before at the onset of their marriage to each other. The parishioners scattered. Many went back to drugs, the street life, and many died. This is why I was called to pray! The wife began to preach out of her bitterness as a traveling evangelist. Much of what she preached was so tainted; it did not resemble the truth at all. The husband, who had actually abdicated his ministerial responsibility to the popular, animated, vocal in-demand wife, became so quiet no one knew where he was. He would never utter a negative word about his wife. He had a crippling fear of her threats and would barely show up to court appearances (even though this writer went). He went into seclusion. He found a multitude of counselors and repented to everyone he saw. The wife succumbed to a gruesome death after an ugly bout with cancer. Now in his sixties, the pastor has married a younger missionary and fathers three more babies, in addition to his four adult children. He is invited to minister at churches, many of which grew out of his original ministerial calling. Needless to say, most everyone had an opinion and expressed it. Some believed he was wrong, and she was justified and vice versa. **He did not let the offenses trap him.** On the other hand, some of the members became members of *The First Church of the Offended,* and had to repent and seek God in order to move forward. It took me twelve years.

In the media, some visible Christian marriages have been the focus, lately. Angry pastor couples are divorcing each other, even in physical altercations. I don't pretend to know their specific issues. They are offended. The root of bitterness had to have been there. The thought came, the hurt followed, went unchecked by the Word. The resulting stronghold was not dealt with. They fell into the trap.

Offences are a trap of the enemy. When we get into hurt, our walk with The Lord is compromised. In offenses, we take our eyes off God. We are attentive to a situation or another person. We may even judge someone else, our job, our church leaders, our family members. When we are caught up in looking at the circumstances, who is praying? One of the enemy's most clever tricks is to get our attention diverted. Then he comes in and steals, kills, and destroys our precious spouses, children, other family, our ministry, our church, our community. God is omniscient and omnipresent. He sees all, knows all and is everywhere and at the same time. He has no hands but our hands, no mouths but our mouths. He wants us to stand in the gap and intercede about everything. "Oh what peace we often forfeit, oh what needless pains we bear. All because we do not carry everything to God in prayer". I do know when all is said and done, God is the Judge, and judges righteously. He is not slack concerning His promises. What He says, He does (2 Peter 3:9)! I know He is Faithful. I know, when we walk in the spirit, we do not fulfill the lust of the flesh. (Gal 5:16).

I had always tried to figure seemingly injustices out and couldn't. But let me go on record as saying, I asked God's forgiveness for judging. I repented for being hurt. I know I have been called to intercede in prayer. Now I am determined to move into the area of blessing others, as God has certainly blessed me. And stay away from the Trap of Offense.

Humbly written by a work in progress,

Bertha Toulson.

October 2007

CHAPTER 15
SPIRITUAL GROWTH 2008

Sometime in the middle of 2008, Bertha and I were invited to a couple's house that we hadn't seen since the Christmas of 2007. While we were there, the couple complained about a couple who they befriended and allowed them to live in their basement for a few months. The couple was in the basement while we were there. Our first question was, have you ask them to leave? They gave us a wimpy answer which basically said "no". We chatted about it for a while and then began talking about other things. We probably stayed there for 90 minutes. Just as were leaving we asked them if we could pray for them and the situation in the basement. Bertha and I prayed and called out the Name of Jesus loud enough I'm sure that they heard us. We get a call the next afternoon from our friends saying that the couple had left first thing in the morning, without saying a word. We told our friends it was because we called out the Name of Jesus, and those demons had to flee.

I few days later, I developed this prayer that I call the **"Jesus Prayer"**.

Jesus Prayer

Jesus, thank you for dying for my sins.

Thank you Jesus for being my Lord and my Savior.

Jesus, thank you that by yours stripes, I am healed.

Thank you Jesus, for being my advocate with my Father.

Jesus, thank you for the examples you left me 2,000 years ago.

When you were baptized in the Jordon and you went into the desert to be tempted by Satan, when he came to you, you didn't argue with him or debate him, you simply said, "It is written...", "It is written...", "It is written ...". And Satan departed you for a season.

Therefore, I can say to Satan and his demon spirits, "The Word of God says …", The Word of God says…", The Word of God says …" , and Satan will depart from me for a season.

Jesus, I thank you that at the Name of Jesus, demons tremble and they have to flee. And because I have your nature, I can walk into any environment, any building, and any room and call out the Name of Jesus and demons tremble and they have to flee.

Jesus, thank you that at the Name of Jesus every knee shall bow and every tongue shall confess that Jesus is Lord!

Jesus, thank you that there in no name above the Name of Jesus. Cancer, stroke, diabetes, heart disease, HIV/AIDS, and any other sickness and disease must bow to the Name of Jesus.

Jesus, thank you for the **POWER** that **I have** in your name!

At the end of the **Spiritual Growth 2005** section, I mentioned that two unctions would take root and begin to bear fruit in my life. In 2007, I began to write down and date what I heard from the Holy Spirit regarding these two unctions. I didn't receive unctions everyday, but I only received them during my early

Morning Prayer time, which was usually between 4-6AM every morning. The piece that I have written entitled, **"Achieving Godly Success"**, is the culmination of the early Morning Prayer thoughts from the Holy Spirit that I wrote down and pondered. I have given out this piece to all 8 of our adult children, some of our spiritual adult children, family and friends. I hope will receive it enjoy it.

Achieving Godly Success

"When a prepared Spirit-filled believer, meets a God-given opportunity, the God-kind of success results." This statement was given to me by the Holy Spirit in the summer of 2005.

In September 2007, the above noted statement began to have much more depth and meaning to me. In September 2007, everything you are about to read started with this note. "When I engage in a **"God-given" opportunity,** as opposed to one I initiate **(a George-hoped-for opportunity)**, that is when the work of my hand is blessed". This led to identifying "opportunities":

<u>**God-given opportunities**</u>

- Marriage to Bertha (May 1995)
- The relationship with my children and grandchildren (May 1995)

- Successful Real Estate Practitioner (January 2002)
- Marriage Ministry (February 2003)
- Graduation from bible school (GWWM School of Biblical Studies) in June 2004

<u>George-hoped-for opportunities</u>

- Executive Training Program (1997)
- Security Watch (Sales job from December 1999 to March 2001)
- CA/DE Investor Project (2006)

The Holy Spirit than had me look at "God-given opportunities". He led me to understand that "God-given opportunities", were from the **Grace of God**. Grace is defined as God's unmerited favor. Grace is a gift from God. Why did I have it? Because I am righteous. I was pre-destined to receive it. God's Grace would be revealed to me by the Holy Spirit.

We have no control over what, when, where, why or how God-given opportunities will manifest themselves.

The Holy Spirit then led me to break down the statement ***"When a prepared Spirit-filled believer, meets a God-given opportunity, the God-kind of success results.***

I. The **first component** is ***"When a prepared Spirit-filled believer ... ".*** How am I prepared?

A) Spiritually Prepared

- Being a doer of God's Word and not a hearer only
- Being obedient to what I hear from the Holy Spirit (God)
- Reading Proverbs 1-31 for each day of the month (daily wisdom)
- Reading Ephesians 1:15-23 and 3:14-21 so that
    - He may grant you ...
- Reading Colossians 1:9-23 so that
    - you may be filled ...
    - you may walk ...
    - you may be invigorated and strengthened

B) Mentally Prepared

- Reading and understanding political issues
- Reading and understanding social issues
- Reading and understanding business issues
- Reading and understanding real estate issues (issues pertaining to my profession; your issues based on your profession will be different)

C) Physically Prepared

- Health
- Dress
- Posture
- Eye contact

What is a **Spirit-filled believer?** A Spirit-filled believer is a person who is filled with the Holy Spirit, with the evidence of speaking in other tongues (scriptural references are noted later in this writing).

If you are, "not prepared", the statement will not work. If you are not a "spirit-filled believer", the statement will not work.

When a **<u>not prepared</u>**, **<u>not spirit-filled believer</u>**, meets a God-given opportunity, the God-kind of success **<u>will not</u>** result!

The following is an important question, and I believe, the correct answer. Going back to the statement *"When a prepared Spirit-filled believer,* when is *"When"*? When is **Today!** The Holy Spirit gave me a powerful revelation about **Today.**

In western cultures, **Today** begins at 12:01AM and ends 12:00 midnight. **Today** is really of a spiritual nature and here is why.

←----------------**Time Past** -------------- **0** ------------**Future Time** ---------------→

Today

Word of Knowledge	**Word of Wisdom**
(Gift of the Holy Spirit)	(Gift of the Holy Spirit)

Today is the time dimension of where a **Word of Knowledge** meets or occupies the same dimension as a **Word of Wisdom!** Webster's dictionary describes **"today"** as "this present day". Webster's describes **"time"** as 1) "the system of those sequential relations that any event has to any other, as past, present, or future; indefinite and continuous duration regarded as that in which events succeed one another. 2. duration regarded as an aspect of the present life distinct from the life to come or from eternity; finite duration". Time can be:

- this second
- this minute
- this hour
- this day
- this week
- this month
- this year
- this decade
- this century
- this millennium

In **Matthew 6:34,** Jesus says, "Take therefore no thought for tomorrow, for tomorrow shall take thought for the things of itself. Sufficient unto today is the evil thereof". The focus should be on **Today.** In **Proverbs 27:1** it says, **"Boast not thyself of tomorrow; for thou knowest not what a day may bring forth".** Again, the focus should be on **Today.**

My Experience with <u>Today</u>

1) About four years ago, I was going to a meeting where I didn't know the outcome of that meeting. I prayed in the spirit (being spirit-filled) on my way to the meeting, and the outcome was better than I expected.

2) Some time after that, maybe a couple of weeks later, I had another opportunity to go into another unknown situation. This time I was very aware that I prayed in the spirit. Again, the outcome was better, much better than I expected.

3) Later, I had another opportunity to go into another unknown situation. This time, I was very, very aware that I prayed in the spirit on my way to this meeting. The outcome of that meeting **far exceeded** my expectations. I rushed home after that meeting, opened the door to my home and shouted, "Honey, I've tapped in!"

I tapped into the Power of the Holy Spirit! I received favorable results **today**, because I prayed in the spirit **today.** In each of the above experiences, I didn't know what I was praying for. In reality, I was praying in faith for a favorable outcome. Now, whenever I go into an unknown situation, which can range from physical, to business, to church, to personal, family, or social relationships, or just going home after a very productive day or a non-productive day, in any venue, I pray in the spirit. And I can report, that **each and every time** I pray in the spirit, the outcome is always better than I could have imagined.

Recently, I took Bertha's car to Pep Boys for an oil change. I also asked them to switch the stop and signal lights on the right side of the car to conform to the left side. They changed the oil but forgot to make the switch. They said it would only take a few more minutes to correct. I said OK, and walked around in the store. While I was walking, I prayed in the spirit, for no other reason than that's what I do when my mind is idle, or I'm going into an unknown situation. This was not an unknown situation, I was just waiting. Well, I'm called and told the car was waiting outside. I went to the counter to pay the bill and I was told, "no charge, sorry to have kept you waiting". I hope you get the point why I pray in the spirit many times during the day. Father, I thank you for the wisdom to know and understand and experience Your Word more perfectly **today**!

II. The Nature of God-given Opportunities

The second component, **"...*meets a God-given opportunity...*"** is about the nature of God-given opportunities that are found in knowing, understanding, and experiencing God's kingdom, or put another way, participating fully in God's economy. Some of the scriptures which **describe** God's economy (or kingdom) are:

A) Deuteronomy 28:1-14 (Blessings)

B) 2 Peter 1: 2-10 (A promise)

C) Malachi 3: 10-12 (Being obedient in tithing)

D) Luke 6:38 (Giving)

E) 2 Corinthians 9: 6-8 (Giving – sowing and reaping)

F) Matthew 6:33 (Seek ye first the kingdom of God and his righteousness …)

G) Proverbs 3: 3-6 (Trust in the Lord with all thine heart …)

H) James 1: 2-4 (… testing of your faith…)

How do I **function** in God's economy? By knowing, understanding, and experiencing the statement, *"When a prepared Spirit-filled believer, meets a God-given opportunity, the God-kind of success results."*

III. Being Spirit-Filled or the Baptism in the Holy Spirit

A) The third component, *"…the God-kind of success results"*, is one of the things in this life we Christians strive to achieve. However, without being **spirit-filled**, even if we are a believer, we are reduced to the world's definition of success, which is "when preparedness meets opportunity, you have success". But it's not the **God-kind** of success! The world's preparedness can be ungodly. For example, stealing, lying, or cheating can prepare you for ungodly opportunities.

B) Being **spirit-filled** requires first **accepting Jesus as your Lord and Savior** by reading, understanding and confessing with your mouth **Romans 10:9-10**. Secondly, by knowing and understanding the following scriptures:

1) Isaiah 28:11-12
2) John 14:16-17, 26
3) Luke 11:9-13
4) Acts 1:8, 2:4, 19:2-6
5) 1 Cor. 14:2, 4, 14
6) Jude 1:20

Get these scriptures in your spirit, then pray this prayer:

Father, I thank you that the moment I ask to be filled with the Holy Sprit, I will be filled. The evidence is that I will speak with other tongues by my will. I will not understand it with my mind. Now, father, fill me with the Holy Spirit, in the Name of Jesus. Thank you for filling me. I have now received. I speak back unto you, by a decision of my will, in other tongues, in the Name of Jesus.

Then begin uttering sounds, which resemble another language. I'd be glad to help anyone with uttering sound. Just call or e-mail me.

Because Jesus died for our sins and became our Lord and Savior, we have access to the Holy Spirit. The Holy Spirit is our power-source is this earth realm.

C) The God-kind of Success

Let's look at an in-depth example of what I believe is the **ultimate "God-kind of Success", Deuteronomy 28: 1-14,** from the King James Version of the bible. I will add some of today's terms (in blue) to make my point.

¹ And it shall come to pass, if thou shalt hearken diligently unto the voice of the LORD thy God, to observe *and* to do all his commandments which I command thee this day, that the LORD thy God will set thee on high above all nations of the earth: ² And all these blessings shall come on thee, and overtake thee, if thou shalt hearken unto the voice of the LORD thy God. ³ Blessed *shalt* thou *be* in the city (where you live), and blessed *shalt* thou *be* in the field (wherever you work). ⁴ Blessed *shall be* the fruit (increase) of thy body, and the fruit (increase) of thy ground (investments) , and the fruit (increase) of thy cattle (investments), the increase of thy kine, and the flocks of thy sheep (investments). ⁵ Blessed *shall be* thy basket (your possessions) and thy store (your business). ⁶ Blessed *shalt* thou *be* when thou comest in, and blessed *shalt* thou *be* when thou goest out (your normal coming and going) . ⁷ The LORD shall cause thine enemies that rise up against thee to be smitten before thy face: they shall come out against thee one way, and flee before thee seven ways. ⁸ The LORD shall command the blessing upon thee in thy storehouses (your house or business building), and in all that thou settest thine hand unto; and he shall bless thee in the land (your territory) which the LORD thy God giveth thee. ⁹ The LORD shall establish thee an holy people unto himself, as he hath sworn unto thee, if thou shalt keep the commandments of the LORD thy God, and walk in his ways. ¹⁰ And all people of the earth shall see that thou art called by the name of the LORD; and they shall be afraid of thee. ¹¹ And the LORD shall make thee plenteous in goods (a lot of material possessions), in the fruit of thy body (children), and in the fruit (increase) of thy cattle (investments), and in the fruit (increase) of thy ground

(investments) , in the land which the LORD sware unto thy fathers to give thee. [12] The LORD shall open unto thee his good treasure (God-given opportunities), the heaven to give the rain unto thy land in his season, and to bless all the work of thine hand: and thou shalt lend unto many nations, and thou shalt not borrow. [13] And the LORD shall make thee the head, and not the tail; and thou shalt be above only, and thou shalt not be beneath; if that thou hearken unto the commandments of the LORD thy God, which I command thee this day, to observe and to do *them*: [14] And thou shalt not go aside from any of the words which I command thee this day, *to* the right hand, or *to* the left, to go after other gods to serve them.

Conclusion

Why did I write this piece? It occurred to me (by unction from the Holy Spirit) that these revelations were not just for me. ***"When a prepared Spirit-filled believer, meets a God-given opportunity, the God-kind of success results."***, is the statement Bertha and I live by everyday. This piece is for those who are **ready to receive it**. You see, it doesn't really matter to me who receives this piece. Of course, I wish everyone who reads this piece would receive it. The only thing that really matters to me is that I was obedient to the Holy Spirit in sharing with you, what he **gave** to me.

George R. Toulson,

CHAPTER 16
SEPTEMBER 2008

As I had mentioned early, Bertha and I became actively involved with the Marriage Fellowship (First Friday) at Victory Christian Fellowship Church. We enjoyed every aspect of the ministry, especially the leadership exhibited from Calvin and Vasanta Wells, the leaders of the ministry. From time to time, Bertha and I would lead a segment of the ministry that particular Friday, or we'd supply the food. In Calvin and Vasanta's absence, Bertha and I would lead to the whole ministry time. Part of any First Friday, is a *"time of sharing"* with the group, where the leaders would impart a message or lead in a group discussion.

This one particular First Friday, Calvin and Vasanta asked us to lead the *"time of sharing"* component, and I read this piece that I had written, and Bertha and I discussed it with the group. The piece is entitled **"The Power of Agreement in Marriage".** We hope you will enjoy it.

The Power of Agreement in Marriage

I. *The Power of Agreement in Marriage*

Let's look at the title of this piece, **"The Power of Agreement in Marriage"**, and examine the key words.

A. What does God's Word say about <u>power</u>?

   Power – There are 424 references of "Power" in the Kings James Version of the bible. However, I believe one verse sums it up perfectly, which is found in Psalms 62:11, which says "...power belongeth unto God."

In **Matthew 16:19,** Jesus is speaking to Peter and he says, "And I will give unto thee the keys of the kingdom and of heaven: and whatsoever thou shalt bind on earth shall be bound in heaven: and whatsoever thou shalt loose on earth shall be loosed in heaven."

As Christians, and as married couples, we have the **POWER** to bind and to loose "whatsoever" in our marriage!

B. What does God's Word say about <u>agreement</u>?

Agreement – In Amos 3:3, God is speaking through the prophet Amos to the people of Israel, saying in verse 3, "Can two walk together, except they be agreed? In other words, God is saying, how can you walk with me, unless you agree with me?

In Matthew 18:19-20, Jesus says, "Again I say unto you, That if two of you shall agree on earth as touching any thing that they shall ask, it shall be done for them of my Father which is in heaven, 20: For where two or three are gathered together in my name, there am I in the midst of them."

In Genesis 11:5-6, it is written, "And the lord came down to see the city and the tower, which the children of men builded. 6: And the lord said, Behold, the people is one, and they have all one language; and they begin to do: and now nothing will be restrained from them, which they have imagined to do."

God, Jesus, and the Holy Spirit, had to come down from heaven to break up the agreement that the people had. For me and my wife, there is no other greater example of the power of agreement. Agreement is a spiritual law.

C. What does God's Word say about <u>marriage</u>?

Marriage – Genesis 2:20-24, it is written, "*20:* And Adam gave names to all cattle, and to the fowl of the air, and to every beast of the field; but for Adam there was not found an help meet for him.
21: And the LORD God caused a deep sleep to fall upon Adam and he slept: and he took one of his ribs, and closed up the flesh instead thereof;
22: And the rib, which the LORD God had taken from man, made he a woman, and brought her unto the man.
23: And Adam said, This is now bone of my bones, and flesh of

my flesh: she shall be called Woman, because she was taken out of Man.

24: Therefore shall a man leave his father and his mother, and shall cleave unto his wife: and they shall be one flesh."

In Proverbs 12:4, it is written, "*4:* A virtuous woman is a crown to her husband: but she that maketh ashamed is as rottenness in his bones. **In Proverbs 18:22, it is written,** "*22:* Whoso findeth a wife findeth a good thing, and obtaineth favour of the LORD. **In Proverbs 31:10, it is written,** "*10:* Who can find a virtuous woman? for her price is far above rubies." **In Ephesians 5:20-31, it is written,** "*20:* Giving thanks always for all things unto God and the Father in the name of our Lord Jesus Christ;

21: Submitting yourselves one to another in the fear of God.

22: Wives, submit yourselves unto your own husbands, as unto the Lord.

23: For the husband is the head of the wife, even as Christ is the head of the church: and he is the saviour of the body.

24: Therefore as the church is subject unto Christ, so let the wives be to their own husbands in every thing.

25: Husbands, love your wives, even as Christ also loved the church, and gave himself for it;

26: That he might sanctify and cleanse it with the washing of water by the word,

27: That he might present it to himself a glorious church, not having spot, or wrinkle, or any such thing; but that it should be holy and without blemish.

28: So ought men to love their wives as their own bodies. He that loveth his wife loveth himself.

29: For no man ever yet hated his own flesh; but nourisheth and cherisheth it, even as the Lord the church:

30: For we are members of his body, of his flesh, and of his bones.

31: For this cause shall a man leave his father and mother, and shall be joined unto his wife, and they two shall be one flesh.

32: This is a great mystery: but I speak concerning Christ and the church.

33: Nevertheless let every one of you in particular so love his wife even as himself; and the wife see that she reverence her husband."

There is a prayer that we have for our unmarried son and two unmarried daughters, that he will find a wife and they will find a husband who loves God more then they love them, and that our son and two daughters will love God more they love their spouses. **This is the recipe for a God-blessed marriage.**

II. The Power and Agreement in Our Marriage

For Bertha and me, our largest segment of agreement in our marriage, is by far our prayer and worship time together each morning between 4-6AM. For the past few years at least, during a typical 30 day month, we may have missed praying together three or four times a month. When Bertha or I are praying, we say, "Yes Father", Yes Jesus, "Yes Holy Spirit", or "Thank You Father", "Thank You Jesus", "Thank You Holy Spirit", in agreement to what the other is praying. We usually read Proverbs for whatever day of the month it happens to be. I read it from the King James Version and Bertha reads it from the Amplified Bible, which adds richness to our reading of Proverbs. I challenge you to read Proverbs each and every day. Bertha and I know that you will experience a difference not only in your marriage, but in your daily aspects of life in relationship with God, yourself, and your fellow man. In our prayer and worship time, we agree that our children and our children's children will come to **know**, and **understand**, and

experience God's Word **more perfectly**, so that they will be **doers of His Word** and not **hearers only.** We agree that other members of our family, friends, colleagues, even people we just met come to know, and understand, and experience God's Word more perfectly, so that they will be doers of His Word and not hearers only. My wife and I agree for good real estate listings, qualified buyers, our new home, and good real estate investments. We agree for marriages everyday, whether it is for a spouse for our unmarried children, couples that are currently married, but are experiencing difficulty in their marriages, or restoration of marriages. My wife and I **NOW** know that we have a marriage ministry.

III. Positive and Negative Powers of Agreement in Marriage

The Holy Spirit quickened my spirit a few years ago, letting me know that there are also negative powers of agreement. Think about it. If the husband or wife talks to another person about their marital situation in a negative way, and that person agrees with them, you have a negative power of agreement. The married person could be totally wrong about a given situation, or partially correct in knowing and understanding the facts of the situation, but now they are in agreement with that other person. Remember I mentioned to you earlier how so powerful the power of agreement was, that God had to come down and change that situation? Agreement with another person about your marital situation, or their marital situation, is still an agreement **for** or **against** your marriage or their marriage. **So, be very careful about what you say regarding another couple's marriage.** Your first response after you have listened to, and had spiritual discernment of the facts (please notice I said spiritual discernment. Ummmm, how do you get that?) should be, **"what does God's Word say about**

that situation?" If you don't know what God's word says about the situation, **shut up**, and refer them to someone who does! **The result of an action or actions based on agreement in marriage or an agreement about a marriage will have the effect of dropping a pebble or a rock in a pond, lake, or ocean. There will be a rippling effect, be it positive or negative, for an unknown period of time!** Let me give you an example of what I believe to be a positive effect in agreement in marriage. A few years ago, I decided that Bertha and I were going to the Gary Whetstone School of Biblical Studies. I was completing the application one evening and Bertha asked me what I was doing. I said, "We are going to bible school." She said OK. That was all she said. She didn't ask how, when, or how much it cost. She had spiritual discernment that let her know that going to bible school was OK (Ummmm, how do you get spiritual discernment?). Well, going to bible school blessed Bertha and me, but we didn't know that our action was instrumental in two other situations. We were at a subsequent **Marriage Advance**, which Victory Christian Fellowship has each year, sitting at the table with two newly wed couples. The couples were Terrance and Theresa, and Daniel and Denise. Theresa and Denise had been in bible school with Bertha and me for most of the two years, and both of them noticed our marriage. They both said to us that we were an example of what they wanted their marriage to be. Here is the point of our power of agreement. I strongly believe had Bertha and I not agreed to go to bible school, or expressed a negative attitude while attending bible school, we probably would not have been sitting at the table with them to hear the positive things they said about our marriage. I believe our power of agreement to attend and graduate from bible school not only produced a rippling effect that affected Theresa's and Denise's marriage, but blessed our marriage mightily in many other ways as well.

IV. If You Don't Like What You Are Receiving

If you don't like what you are **receiving** from your spouse, check on what you have been **giving** your spouse.

V. Your Marriage Is the Biggest Game Trophy Satan Can Get

There are only two institutions that God ordained – Marriage and the Church. Therefore, it stands to reason that Satan will bring all of his God-given power to bear against these two institutions. In Daniel 7:25, it is written "*25:* And he (Satan) shall speak great words against the most High, and shall wear out the saints of the most High, and think to change times and laws: and they shall be given into his hand until a time and times and the dividing of time. However, in Ephesians 6:10-18, Paul writes "*10:* Finally, my brethren, be strong in the Lord, and in the power of his might.
11: Put on the whole armor of God, that ye may be able to stand against the wiles of the devil.

12: For we wrestle not against flesh and blood, but against principalities, against powers, against the rulers of the darkness of this world, against spiritual wickedness in high places.
13: Wherefore take unto you the whole armor of God, that ye may be able to withstand in the evil day, and having done all, to stand.
14: Stand therefore, having your loins girt about with truth, and having on the breastplate of righteousness;
15: And your feet shod with the preparation of the gospel of peace;
16: Above all, taking the shield of faith, wherewith ye shall be able to quench all the fiery darts of the wicked.
17: And take the helmet of salvation, and the sword of the

Spirit, which is the word of God:

18: Praying always with all prayer and supplication in the Spirit, and watching thereunto with all perseverance and supplication for all saints;

Dr. Betty Price of Crenshaw Christian Center, where we fellowshipped before coming to Victory Christian Fellowship, would say, be of one accord, one mind, one spirit, speaking the same thing, serving God, that we may come into the unity of the faith, and the fullness of the stature of Christ. She would say this addressing the congregation at Crenshaw Christian Center. ***My wife and I say this to you, married couples, be of one accord, one mind, one spirit, speaking the same thing, serving God, that you may come into the unity of the faith, and the fullness of the stature of Christ.***

Don't allow Satan to hang your marriage on his trophy wall!!!

Be in **Agreement** for a God-blessed marriage. **God Bless You!**

Marriage Scriptures	Financial Scriptures	Faith Scriptures
I Corinthians 13	Malachi 3: 8-12	Hebrews 11: 1, 3, 6
Ephesians 5: 22-33	Luke 6: 38	Philippians 4: 13, 19
I Peter 3: 1-2, 7	2 Corinthians 9: 6-8	
Genesis 2: 21-24		
Deuteronomy 28: 1-14		

George R. Toulson, Sr.

November 2008

Spiritual Growth 2009

The year 2009, the last year in this decade, would prove very challenging, but by standing on God's promises, Bertha and I went through those challenges. There were many times I spoke *James 1:2-4* which reads, *² My brethren, count it all joy when you fall into various trials, ³ knowing that the testing of your faith produces patience. ⁴ But let patience have its perfect work, that you may be perfect and complete, lacking nothing.* [9]

In January 2009, the economy was at it lowest since the Great Depression in 1929. Millions of jobs had been lost in the past 12 months, and the real estate market, which provided our livelihood, which peaked in May 2006, was at its worst in terms of depressed housing prices, and the market was flooded with properties in all price ranges. Many homeowners, without a job, or a spouse who lost their job, just walked away from their homes, adding to the homes already on the market, and depressed home values even more. This was certainly a buyer's market for those who could buy. But with so many homes on the market, those buyers were taking their time, with so many homes to choose from, and offering in many cases, ridiculously low offers, which made working with some buyers very difficult. Naturally, sellers were having a difficult time as well. They couldn't buy their next home, because they couldn't sell

---

[9] *The New King James Version.* 1996, c1982 . Thomas Nelson: Nashville

their current home. Couple that with mortgage lenders tightening their credit standards. Plus, the mortgage underwriting process becoming more stringent in its requirements, made the residential real estate profession additionally challenging.

James 1:2-4 was uttered from my mouth often in 2009, but God continued to bless Bertha and me. In January, we visited my son Charles in Texas and stayed at his very large, new home near Dallas. We toured his orthopedic practice in near Dallas, where he had his own orthopedic wing of the hospital. In February, we went to Arizona to visit Bertha's oldest son Zane and his wife Jolee. Zane and Jolee were looking at building a multi multi-million dollar sports complex and Bertha and I went there to be in agreement with them and their investors in buying the necessary land. While in Arizona, we visited the Grand Canyon, in all it's splendor. That was a **WOW** moment! Another one of God's wonders!

At the end of February, Bertha and I lead a break-out session at ***Victory Christian Fellowship's 2009 Marriage Advance*** in Ocean City, MD. We spoke on the subject, "**Power of Agreement in Marriage**". The break-out session was very well attended and our talk and group discussion was very well received. Later that afternoon, in the Main Ballroom session of the Advance, Bertha and I were asked to participate with Pastor Gary and Pastor Faye in an open forum to discuss whatever questions came from the Marriage Advance audience. Bertha and I truly appreciated the acknowledgement of our marriage in being asked to participate in the open forum.

On April 30th, in celebration of our 14th wedding anniversary on May 6th, we went on our 2nd Caribbean cruise (8 day) on the cruise ship Carnival Miracle out of New York City. We paid cash. This time we traveled to San Juan, St. Thomas and Grand Turk. While on this cruise, I spoke with cruise personnel about missing our 2007 Mexican Riviera cruise because of my mother's death. Carnival was gracious enough to give us a replacement cruise that we would take approximately 7 weeks later. **What a fantastic blessing from God!** For this cruise, we flew to Los Angeles, spent a few days with friends and family, than got aboard the Carnival Splendor on June 21st for a 7 day Mexican Riviera cruise. Our ports of call were Puerto Vallarta, Mazatian, and Cabo San Lucas, Mexico.

In between these two cruises, my beloved Pastor, Charles E. Waters, III went home to be with the Lord on May 24, 2009. As soon as I heard he had passed, I asked his wife Mary if I could say a few words at his going home celebration. This man truly saved my life when he agreed with me for deliverance from alcohol, and I had to publically acknowledge what he did for me. When it was my turn to speak, I prefaced my comments by saying; you never know whose life you may impact, or who God will put in your path. Pastor Waters was truly a great man and I'll always remember him and be thankful to God for him.

The second half of 2009 was rough on us financially because of the depressed real estate market. The real estate market caused many real estate brokerage firms to close offices, including our Weichert Office in Wilmington. All associates were reassigned to our Pike Creek office, 11.5 miles away.

Many of the associates in the Wilmington office lived less than 10 minutes from the Wilmington office, so driving to the Pike Creek office caused many of them join other real estate brokerage firms near the old Wilmington office. The Pike Creek office was closer to where Bertha and I lived, so the relocation was a blessing to us.

In September, two real estate transactions, that were scheduled to close, didn't. One buyer had cold feet regarding a home inspection issue and refused to move forward with the transaction, even though the seller agreed to fix the issue. The second buyer switched jobs in her company. She went from a salaried position to a commission position, and the mortgage underwriting process said she had to demonstrate that she could earn the same on commission as she earned on salary and they denied her loan. She will be able to get a mortgage in February of 2010. In the meantime, she and her husband started coming to our Marriage Fellowship in November.

These two transactions made it such that there was no income for about 8 weeks coming from our real estate business, but where God guides, He provides, and all of our need was met. Thank you *James 1:2-4!*

First Friday, November 2009

I mentioned massaging Bertha at our First Friday event. We had a lot fun with that topic and there was a lot of group discussion. During and after the event, many of the wives thanked Bertha and me for bringing up the topic. For a few weeks after the First Friday event, many of the husbands that were in attendance would see me and smile and gesture with their hands that massaging was working for them. Here is my opinion (Bertha agrees) on massaging.

Massaging

A few years after we were married, Bertha and I were watching a National Geographic program where snow monkeys in Japan were grooming each other. The monkeys were making sure that each others coat was free from debris and insects. Excuse the pun, but it was touching.

Watching the grooming gave you a sense of caring among the monkey and I actually thought about Bertha. Don't I love her so much that I'd want her skin to look as perfect as possible, to have a glow about it? Of course I do. Which lead me to putting lotion on her skin, often times after she took a bath. While applying the lotion, I'd apply some pressure, which felt good to her by the sounds she was making, and I noted what I was hearing in my mind. I quickly understood that touching Bertha is a **loving act**. When touching is done carefully, it is deliberate and thought provoking.

Thought provoking you might ask? How so? How many times have you wanted to accomplish something but you needed others cooperation, assistance or permission? For example, if I want a real estate transaction to close, I have to find a willing and able buyer. We then have to find a suitable property. Once we've found a suitable property, we then have to negotiate with the seller on price and terms. Once price and terms are agreed, the mortgage underwriting process takes place, and given all underwriting criteria is satisfied, the loan is granted and the buyer then acquires the property. When massaging my wife or my wife massaging me, it's just me and her. If I'm attentive to her needs and listen to how she responds, I can bring **creativity** (thought provoking) into the massaging process for a more effective and efficient experience.

How do I ask again? Four questions come to mind. *How* will I massage her? *Where* on her body will I massage her? *How long* will I massage her? What will be the *frequency* of her massages? For me, the fun part is thinking and doing whatever, being creative. Here is my take on these four questions. Hopefully, your take may or may not be different. If you feel you're not the creative sort, do what I do here and watch your creativity grow.

How

What parts of your hand(s) will you use? You've got one hand or two hands, your whole hand, your fingers, the tips of your fingers, the palm of your hand, and the knuckles. You can use your hand(s) to rub, squeeze the muscle and skin using the thumb and four fingers, use your knuckles, use clockwise and counter-clockwise motion, with varying degrees of pressure. You can use the edge of your hand(s) in a judo-chop fashion, with varying degrees of impact. You can us your wrists, forearms, elbows, and feet. Ask her would she prefer her favorite oil or lotion. Men, two very important things; Make sure you hands are clean and smooth, not like sand paper, or you won't get to first base. Get a pumice stone and use it on your hands prior to the massage. Also, use petroleum jelly on your hands. In my opinion, it works better than any kind of lotion or oil.

Where

I believe anywhere on her body that you start will be OK and appreciated. Remember, I rubbed Bertha's feet when we first met? At the time, I had no idea of the impact that would make. But, I further believe your goal should be from the **top of her head** to the **souls of her feet.** Don't be surprised that the first few times you do this, you put her to sleep, which might not be the ultimate goal, but she will awake. The first time Bertha massaged me from the bottom of my feet to the top of my head, I was asleep before she got to my butt. That was way to much control.

How Long

However long it takes to go from the **top of her head** to the **soles of her feet.** I believe that *slow* and *deliberate* should be your mindset. Of course, I've timed myself on various occasions to gather intelligence for later *missions*. Sometimes the *mission* at hand gets side-tracked for your benefit. However, the *mission* can be sabotaged if you haven't turned off your cell phones or the house phone rings.

Frequency

For a **top of her head** to the **soles of her feet** massage, I believe a minimum of at least once a week is required. Anything less than a full body massage can be done several times a week, even daily.

Additional Benefits

In addition to massaging of muscles, the consistent rubbing and squeezing of the skin, using lotion or oil produces tightness, a smoothing, and a glowing of the skin. And you the massager get the benefit of firming the muscles in your hands, forearms, biceps, triceps, and shoulders.

If slow, deliberate, and loving is your mindset, over a period of time, you will discover the massaging pattern(s) which brings the most satisfaction to your spouse.

Massaging can be foreplay **before** the foreplay!

Remember, massaging is a loving act. You can do whatever is pleasing to your wife or husband. The only thing that's stopping you is your creativity. I never read a book or gone online for advice. I didn't and don't need to. I've got the Holy Spirit to guide me every step of the way.

A Word of Caution

Here is a parable. Massaging is like detailing your vehicle, and we know the effort that goes into detailing a vehicle. Detailing your vehicle is not going to occur if there's no gas in the vehicle. Detailing your vehicle is not going to occur if the engine needs a tune-up. Detailing your vehicle is not going to occur if the transmission is not working properly. And detailing your vehicle is not going to occur if the tires are bad.

Your vehicle in this parable is your marriage. Massaging is not going to occur if there are financial issues in your marriage. Massaging is not going to occur if there is disagreement in your marriage. Massaging is not going to occur if there is disrespect in your marriage. And massaging is not going to occur if there is any kind of strife in your marriage.

Spiritual Growth 2010

The seed of this book was probably planted in 1995 after Bertha and I were married. Even then, in my faith infancy, I knew what God had done and was doing in our lives was truly an abundant blessing. This was the happiest time of our lives. In December 2008, I sat down and began to write. I didn't have an outline, I just wrote. What I did have were the letters, poems, and post cards I wrote and sent to Bertha beginning in June 1994, and her letters and post cards she wrote and mailed to me. But the most important thing I possessed was the **Holy Spirit** guiding me along on this blessed journey from 1995 to 2010. After writing several pages, the title came to me **"Our Marriage – Our Redemption"**.

The title seemed appropriate because through our almost 15 years of marriage, all that Bertha and I had missed out on, whether our fault or the fault of others previous to our marriage, God restored all of that and much more. Our marriage has provided the framework for all that you have read in this book so far.

Bertha and I will continue to strive to know and understand and experience **God's Word** more perfectly, so that we will be doers of His Word and not hearers only. We will continue to have the passion we have for marriages, and our spirits will always be ready, willing, and able to allow the Holy Spirit to flow through us to meet the needs of God's people.

This book is really not about George and Bertha. This book is about **God's Glory.** God could have used any two people from the hundreds of millions of eligible people that inhabit this planet to deliver this story of marriage and redemption. Bertha and I know that God has used countless stories throughout history to get His Glory. We are truly blessed and honored to tell our humble story. My prayer all along has been that this book be a blessing to the Body of Christ. Not only for those that are married, but also for those that want to be married.

I know that for me, back in 1994, I had zero expectations, none! As we approach our 15th wedding anniversary, and I plan for our wedding anniversary cruise, Bertha and I can summarize our expectations as this – *God knows our needs and God knows our desires, and we trust Him.* **Proverbs 3:5-6** sums it up perfectly. It says, ***"Trust in the Lord with all thine heart and lean not unto thine own understanding. In all thy ways acknowledge him and he shall direct thy paths.***

Thank you Father *for allowing us to convey Your Glory through us with whoever reads this book.*

George & Bertha Toulson

246

Index of Prayers

Adoration Prayer

Doer and Hearer Prayer

Functioning in God's Economy Prayer

Health and Marriage Prayer

Holy Spirit Prayer

Jesus Prayer

Spiritual Foundation Prayer

Spiritual Warfare Prayer

Adoration Prayer

Heavenly Father, I praise your name.

Father, I give you praise, I give you glory, I give you honor. I give you adoration,

I give you thanksgiving.

Father, I worship you and I adore you because I know who you are.

You are ***Jehovah-Jireh***, the One who sees my needs and provides for them. Hallowed be Thy Name!

You are ***El-Shaddai***, the God Almighty of blessings. You are the Breasty One Who nourishes and supplies. You are all-bountiful and you are all-sufficient. Hallowed be Thy Name!

You are ***Jehovah-Shalom***. You are my Peace. The peace that transcends all understanding. Hallowed be Thy Name!

Father, I know your 12 redemptive names. I know your character. And because I know you, I have access to you.

Thank you Father, In Jesus Name!

The greatest thing in the life we live is **salvation**! With salvation comes God's character. However, if you don't know God's character, you will miss out on what you have access to.

Doer and Hearer Prayer

For Adults

Father, we thank you that ________ would come to **know** and **understand** and **experience** your *Word* more **perfectly,** so that he/she would be a **doer** of your Word and not a **hearer** only *(James 1:22)*. We pray that his/her **experiences** will be part of their **testimony** and that they will **serve** you.

For Teenagers and Children

Father, we thank you that ________ would come to **know** and **understand** and **experience** your *Word* at an **early age** so that he/she would be a **doer** of your Word and not a **hearer** only. We pray that his/her **experiences** will be part of their **testimony** and that they will **serve** you.

Functioning in God's Economy

Father, I thank you that I function in your economy, not the world's economy. Holy Spirit, I thank you for showing me scriptures that **describe** God's economy.

A) Deuteronomy 28:1-14 *(Blessings)*

B) 2 Peter 1: 2-10 *(A promise)*

C) Malachi 3: 10-12 *(Being obedient in tithing)*

D) Luke 6:38 *(Giving)*

E) 2 Corinthians 9: 6-8 *(Giving – sowing and reaping)*

F) Matthew 6:33 *(Seek ye first the kingdom of God and his righteousness ...)*

G) Proverbs 3: 3-6 *(Trust in the Lord with all thine heart ...)*

H) James 1: 2-4 *(... testing of your faith...)*

Holy Spirit, I thank you for showing me how to **function** in God's economy by knowing, understanding, and experiencing the statement, *"When a prepared Spirit-filled believer, meets a God-given opportunity, the God-kind of success results."*

Father, I thank you that I function in your economy, in the Name of Jesus!

Health & Marriage Prayer

Father, my wife and I thank you for this day.

I thank you for my health and for my strength. I thank you for renewing my mind and my body.

I thank you that I am healed from the top of my head, to the soles of my feet.

I thank you that there are no stroke symptoms, there are no HIV, there are no AIDS, there are no cancerous cells in my body.

I thank you that I have a very strong heart and that each and every cell is operating as You designed it.

Father, I thank you for my wife. I thank you for her love. I thank you for her health and for her strength.

I thank you for renewing her mind and her body.

I thank you that she is healed from the top of her head to the soles of her feet.

I thank you that there are no stroke symptoms, there are no HIV, there are no AIDS, there are no cancerous cells in her body.

I thank you that she has a very strong heart and that each and every cell is operating as You designed it.

Father, I thank you for our marriage and our sweet and tender love making, and I believe it will continue for many, many, many, many, many, many, many more years in the Name of Jesus.

Holy Spirit Prayer

Father, I thank you for your **Word**, for your **Word** is truth and your **Word** is life, and it will not return unto you void, but will accomplish your divine decree. (Isaiah 55:11)

Father, I thank you that your **Word** declares that greater is **He** that lives in me then he that is in the world. (1 John 4:4)

Holy Spirit, I thank you for **teaching me the things of God** and **bringing all things to my remembrance.** (John 14: 26)

Holy Spirit, I thank you for **dwelling in me and for comforting me** (John 14: 17, John 14:26).

I thank you for guiding me in all that I say and in all that I do. Because Holy Spirit I know, that by standing on God's Word and with your guidance, I will rise above all situations and all circumstances (my financial situation, my credit situation, and my tax situation) and I will be victorious in all that I set my hands to.

Holy Spirit, my human spirit is tapped into you. I thank you for opening my heart and my mind. Speak to me Holy Spirit, whether it be through an audible voice, unctions, or the Word of God. I desperately need to hear from you **TODAY**

Jesus Prayer

Jesus, thank you for dying for my sins.

Thank you for being my Lord and my Savior.

Jesus, thank you that by yours stripes, I am healed.

Thank you for being my advocate with my Father.

Jesus, thank you for the examples you left me 2,000 years ago.

When you were baptized in the Jordan and you went into the desert to be tempted by Satan, when he came to you, you didn't argue with him or debate him, you simply said, "It is written...", "It is written...", "It is written ...". And Satan departed him for a season.

Therefore, I can say to Satan and his demon spirits, "The Word of God says ...", The Word of God says...", The Word of God says ...", and Satan will depart from me for a season.

Jesus, I thank you that at the Name of Jesus, demons tremble and they have to flee. And because I have your nature, I can walk into any environment, any building, and any room and call out the Name of Jesus and demons tremble and they have to flee.

Jesus, thank you that at the Name of Jesus every knee shall bow and every tongue shall confess that Jesus is Lord!

Jesus, thank you that there in no name above the Name of Jesus. Cancer, stroke, diabetes, heart disease, HIV/AIDS, and any other sickness and disease must bow to the Name of Jesus.

Jesus, thank you for the **POWER** that **I have** in your name!

Spiritual Foundation Prayer

Father, I thank you for **sustaining** us.

Father, I thank you for allowing us to **abide under your shadow**.

Father, I thank you that you are **faithful.**

Father, I thank you that **all of our need is met**, according to your riches in glory by Christ Jesus.

I thank you Dear God that I am **focused on the promises** that are in Deuteronomy 28:1-14 and not the circumstances:

> I will not be moved by how I feel or don't feel, for those are circumstances and distractions.

> I will not be moved by what I see or don't see, for those are circumstances and distractions.

I will not be moved by what I hear or don't hear, for those are circumstances and distractions.

I am only moved the Spirit of the Living God!

I thank you Dear God that **no weapon formed against** me, my wife, or our family shall prosper, and every tongue that rises up in judgment against us, we shall condemn.

I thank you Dear God that you have **not given me the spirit of fear,** but the spirit of power, and of love, and of a sound mind.

Spiritual Warfare Prayer

Father, I thank you for your **Word**, for your **Word** is truth and your **Word** is life, and it will not return unto you void, but will accomplish your divine decree. (Isaiah 55:11)

Father, I thank you that your **Word** declares that greater is **He** that lives in me then he that is in the world. (1 John 4:4)

Father, I thank you that at the **Name of Jesus**, every knee shall bow and every tongue shall confess that Jesus is Lord! (Romans 14:11)

Father, I thank you that your **Word** declares that I am above only and not beneath, that I am the head and not the tail, that I have right standing. (Deuteronomy 28: 13)

Father, I thank you that your **Word** declares that whatsoever I bind on earth is bound in heaven, and whatsoever I loose on earth is loosed in heaven. (Matthew 16: 19)

Therefore Satan, you and your demon spirits, I come against you with the same **Holy Spirit Power** that raised Jesus from the dead. You have no authority over me, my wife, or our families in the Name of Jesus.

Satan, you and your demon spirits, the **Word of God** *says* that greater is **He** that is in me then he that is in the world.

Satan, you and your demon spirits, the **Word of God** *says* that I am above only and not beneath, that I am the head and not the tail, that I have right standing.

Satan, you and your demon spirits, the **Word of God** *says* that whatsoever I bind on earth is bound in heaven and whatsoever I loose on earth is loosed in heaven.

Therefore Satan, you and your demon spirits, I **bind** and **rebuke** all of your **financial maneuvers and strategies** against me, my wife and our families in the Name of Jesus, and I **command** you to **loose** all of your **financial assignments** against me, my wife, and our families in the Name of Jesus!

Satan, you and your demon spirits, I **bind** and **rebuke** all of your **business maneuvers and strategies** against me, my wife and our families in the Name of Jesus, and I **command** you to **loose** all of your **business assignments** against me, my wife, and our families in the Name of Jesus!

Satan, you and your demon spirits, I **bind** and **rebuke** all of your **legal maneuvers and strategies** against me, my wife and our families in the Name of Jesus, and I **command** you to **loose** all of your **legal assignments** against me, my wife, and our families in the Name of Jesus!

Satan, you and your demon spirits, I **bind** and **rebuke** all of your **marriage maneuvers and strategies** against me, my wife and our families in the Name of Jesus, and I **command** you to **loose** all of your **marriage assignments** against me, my wife, and our families in the Name of Jesus!

Satan, you and your demon spirits, I **bind** and **rebuke** all of your **personal maneuvers and strategies** against me, my wife and our families in the Name of Jesus, and I **command** you to **loose** all of your **personal assignments** against me, my wife, and our families in the Name of Jesus!

Satan, you and your demon spirits, I **bind** and **rebuke** all of your **mechanical maneuvers and strategies** against me, my wife and our families in the Name of Jesus, and I **command** you to **loose** all of your **mechanical assignments** against me, my wife, and our families in the Name of Jesus!

Satan, you and your demon spirits, I **bind** and **rebuke** all of your **health maneuvers and strategies** against me, my wife and our families in the Name of Jesus, and I **command** you to **loose** all of your **health assignments** against me, my wife, and our families in the Name of Jesus!

Father, I thank you for **loosing** all of your **ministering spirits** to provide for me, my wife and our families with all of our **needs and desires** in the Name of Jesus!

Index of Spiritual Writings

Achieving Godly Success

How Long Is Eternity?

The Power of Agreement in Marriage

Traps of the Offended

What Are You Thinking About?

Achieving Godly Success

"When a prepared Spirit-filled believer, meets a God-given opportunity, the God-kind of success results." This statement was given to me by the Holy Spirit in the summer of 2005.

In September 2007, the above noted statement began to have much more depth and meaning to me. In September 2007, everything you are about to read started with this note. "When I engage in a **"God-given" opportunity,** as opposed to one I initiate (a George-hoped-for opportunity), that is when the work of my hand is blessed". This led to identifying "opportunities":

<u>God-given opportunities</u>

- Marriage to Bertha (May 1995)
- The relationship with my children and grandchildren (May 1995)
- Successful Real Estate Practitioner (January 2002)
- Marriage Ministry (February 2003)
- Graduation from bible school (GWWM School of Biblical Studies) in June 2004

<u>George-hoped-for opportunities</u>

- Executive Training Program (1997)
- Security Watch (Sales job from December 1999 to March 2001)
- CA/DE Investor Project (2006)

The Holy Spirit then had me look at "God-given opportunities". He led me to understand that "God-given opportunities" were from the **Grace of God**. Grace is defined as God's unmerited favor. Grace is a gift from God. Why did I have it? Because I am righteous. I was pre-destined to receive it. God's Grace would be revealed to me by the Holy Spirit.

We have no control over what, when, where, why or how God-given opportunities will manifest themselves. We do have control over the statement, **"When a prepared Spirit-filled believer, meets a God-given opportunity, the God-kind of success results."**

The Holy Spirit then led me to break down the statement *"When a prepared Spirit-filled believer, meets a God-given opportunity, the God-kind of success results.*

I. The **first component** is *"When a prepared Spirit-filled believer ... ".* How am I prepared?

A) Spiritually Prepared

- Being a doer of God's Word and not a hearer only

- Being obedient to what I hear from the Holy Spirit (God)
- Reading Proverbs 1-31 for each day of the month (daily wisdom)
- Reading Ephesians 1:15-23 and 3:14-21 so that
    - He may grant you ...
- Reading Colossians 1:9-23 so that
    - you may be filled ...
    - you may walk ...
    - you may be invigorated and strengthened

B) Mentally Prepared

- Reading and understanding political issues
- Reading and understanding social issues
- Reading and understanding business issues
- Reading and understanding real estate issues (issues pertaining to my profession, your issues based on your profession will be different)

C) Physically Prepared

- Health
- Dress
- Posture
- Eye contact

What is a **Spirit-filled believer?** A Spirit-filled believer is a person who is filled with the Holy Spirit, with the evidence of speaking in other tongues (scriptural references are noted later in this writing).

If you are "not prepared", the statement will not work. If you are not a "spirit-filled believer", the statement will not work.

When a **<u>not prepared</u>**, **<u>not spirit-filled believer</u>**, meets a God-given opportunity, the God-kind of success **<u>will not</u>** result!

The following is an important question, and I believe, the correct answer. Going back to the statement ***"When a prepared Spirit-filled believer,*** when is ***"When"?*** When is **Today!** The Holy Spirit gave me a powerful revelation about **Today.**

In western cultures, **Today** begins at 12:01AM and ends 12:00 midnight. **Today** is really of a spiritual nature and here is why.

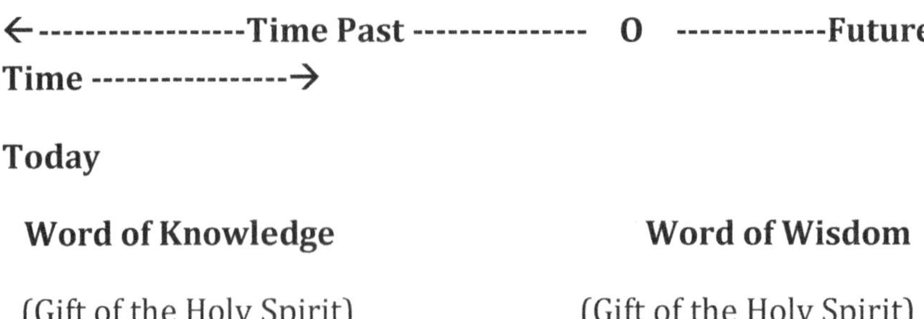

Today is the time dimension of where a **Word of Knowledge** meets or occupies the same dimension as a **Word of Wisdom!** Webster's dictionary describes **"today"** as "this present day". Webster's describes **"time"** as 1) "the system of those sequential relations that any event has to any other, as past, present, or future; indefinite and continuous duration regarded as that in which events succeed one another. 2. duration regarded as an aspect of the present life distinct from the life to come or from eternity; finite duration". Time can be:

- this second
- this minute
- this hour
- this day
- this week
- this month
- this year
- this decade
- this century
- this millennium

In **Matthew 6:34,** Jesus says, "Take therefore no thought for tomorrow, for tomorrow shall take thought for the things of itself. Sufficient unto today is the evil thereof". The focus should be on **Today.** In **Proverbs 27:1** it says, **"Boast not thyself of tomorrow; for thou knowest not what a day may bring forth".** Again, the focus should be on **Today.**

My Experience with <u>Today</u>

4) About three years ago, I was going to a meeting where I didn't know the outcome of that meeting. I prayed in the

spirit (being spirit-filled) on my way to the meeting, and the outcome was better than I expected.

5) Some time after that, maybe a couple of weeks later, I had another opportunity to go into another unknown situation. This time I was very aware that I prayed in the spirit. Again, the outcome was better, much better than I expected.

6) Later, I had another opportunity to go into another unknown situation. This time, I was very, very aware that I prayed in the spirit on my way to this meeting. The outcome of that meeting **far exceeded** my expectations. I rushed home after that meeting, opened the door to my home and shouted, "Honey, I've tapped in!"

I tapped into the power of the Holy Spirit! I received favorable results **today**, because I prayed in the spirit **today.** In each of the above experiences, I didn't know what I was praying for. In reality, I was praying in faith for a favorable outcome. Now, whenever I go into an unknown situation, which can range from physical, to business, to church, to personal, family, or social relationships, or just going home after a very productive day or a non-productive day, in any venue, I pray in the spirit. And I can report, that **each and every time** I pray in the spirit, the outcome is always better than I could have imagined.

Recently, I took Bertha's car to Pep Boys for an oil change. I also asked them to switch the stop and signal lights on the right side of the car to conform to the left side. They changed the oil but forgot to make the switch. They said it would only take a few more minutes to correct. I said OK, and walked around in the store. While I was walking, I prayed in the spirit, for no other reason than that's what I do when my mind is idle, or I'm going into an unknown situation. This was not an unknown situation, I was just waiting. Well, I'm called and told the car was waiting outside. I went to the counter to pay the bill and I was told, "no charge, sorry to have kept you waiting". I hope you get the point why I pray in the spirit many times during the day. Father, I thank you for the wisdom to know and understand and experience Your Word more perfectly **today**!

II. The Nature of God-given Opportunities

The second component, "...*meets a God-given opportunity...*" is about the nature of God-given opportunities that are found in knowing, understanding, and experiencing God's kingdom, or put another way, participating fully in God's economy. Some of the scriptures which **describe** God's economy (or kingdom) are:

A) Deuteronomy 28:1-14 (Blessings)

B) 2 Peter 1: 2-10 (A promise)

C) Malachi 3: 10-12 (Being obedient in tithing)

D) Luke 6:38 (Giving)

E) 2 Corinthians 9: 6-8 (Giving – sowing and reaping)

F) Matthew 6:33 (Seek ye first the kingdom of God and his righteousness ...)

G) Proverbs 3: 3-6 (Trust in the Lord with all thine heart ...)

H) James 1: 2-4 (... testing of your faith...)

How do I **<u>function</u>** in God's economy? By knowing, understanding, and experiencing the statement, ***"When a prepared Spirit-filled believer, meets a God-given opportunity, the God-kind of success results."***

III. Being Spirit-Filled or the Baptism in the Holy Spirit

A) The third component, ***"...the God-kind of success results"***, is one of the things in this life we Christians strive to achieve. However, without being **spirit-filled**, even if we are a believer, we are reduced to the world's definition of success, which is "when preparedness meets opportunity, you have success". But it's not the **God-kind** of success! The world's preparedness can be ungodly. For example, stealing, lying, or cheating can prepare you for ungodly opportunities.

B) Being **spirit-filled** requires first **accepting Jesus as your Lord and Savior** by reading, understanding and confessing with your mouth **Romans 10:9-10**. Secondly, by knowing and understanding the following scriptures:

   7) Isaiah 28:11-12
   8) John 14:16-17, 26
   9) Luke 11:9-13
   10)Acts 1:8, 2:4, 19:2-6

11)1 Cor. 14:2, 4, 14
12)Jude 1:20

Get these scriptures in your spirit, then pray this prayer:

Father, I thank you that the moment I ask to be filled with the Holy Sprit, I will be filled. The evidence is that I will speak with other tongues by my will. I will not understand it with my mind. Now, father, fill me with the Holy Spirit, in the Name of Jesus. Thank you for filling me. I have now received. I speak back unto you, by a decision of my will, in other tongues, in the Name of Jesus.

Then begin uttering sounds, which resemble another language. I'd be glad to help anyone with uttering sound. Just call or e-mail me.

Because Jesus died for our sins and became our Lord and Savior, we have access to the Holy Spirit. The Holy Spirit is our power-source is this earth realm.

C) The God-kind of Success

Let's look at an in-depth example of what I believe is the **ultimate "God-kind of Success", Deuteronomy 28: 1-14**, from the King James version of the bible. I will add some of today's terms (in blue) to make my point.

¹ And it shall come to pass, if thou shalt hearken diligently unto the voice of the LORD thy God, to observe *and* to do all his commandments which I command thee this day, that the LORD thy God will set thee on high above all nations of the earth: ² And all these blessings shall come on thee, and overtake thee, if thou shalt hearken unto the voice of the LORD thy God. ³ Blessed *shalt* thou *be* in the city (where you live), and blessed *shalt* thou *be* in the field (wherever you work). ⁴ Blessed *shall be* the fruit (increase) of thy body, and the fruit (increase) of thy ground (investments) , and the fruit (increase) of thy cattle (investments), the increase of thy kine, and the flocks of thy sheep (investments). ⁵ Blessed *shall be* thy basket (your possessions) and thy store (your business). ⁶ Blessed *shalt* thou *be* when thou comest in, and blessed *shalt* thou *be* when thou goest out (your normal coming and going) . ⁷ The LORD shall cause thine enemies that rise up against thee to be smitten before thy face: they shall come out against thee one way, and flee before thee seven ways. ⁸ The LORD shall command the blessing upon thee in thy storehouses (your house or business building), and in all that thou settest thine hand unto; and he shall bless thee in the land (your territory) which the LORD thy God giveth thee. ⁹ The LORD shall establish thee an holy people unto himself, as he hath sworn unto thee, if thou shalt keep the commandments of the LORD thy God, and walk in his ways. ¹⁰ And all people of the earth shall see that thou art called by the name of the LORD; and they shall be afraid of thee. ¹¹ And the LORD shall make thee plenteous in goods (a lot of material possessions), in the fruit of thy body (children), and in the fruit (increase) of thy cattle (investments), and in the fruit (increase) of thy ground

(investments) , in the land which the LORD sware unto thy fathers to give thee. [12] The LORD shall open unto thee his good treasure (God-given opportunities), the heaven to give the rain unto thy land in his season, and to bless all the work of thine hand: and thou shalt lend unto many nations, and thou shalt not borrow. [13] And the LORD shall make thee the head, and not the tail; and thou shalt be above only, and thou shalt not be beneath; if that thou hearken unto the commandments of the LORD thy God, which I command thee this day, to observe and to do *them*: [14] And thou shalt not go aside from any of the words which I command thee this day, *to* the right hand, or *to* the left, to go after other gods to serve them.

Conclusion

Why did I write this piece? It occurred to me (by unction from the Holy Spirit) that these revelations were not just for me. ***"When a prepared Spirit-filled believer, meets a God-given opportunity, the God-kind of success results."***, is the statement Bertha and I live by everyday. This piece is for those who are **ready to receive it**. You see, it doesn't really matter to me who receives this piece. Of course, I wish everyone who reads this piece would receive it. The only thing that really matters to me is that I was obedient to the Holy Spirit in sharing with you, what he **gave** to me.

George R. Toulson, Sr.

September 2008

How Long is Eternity?

How long is eternity? In Isaiah 57:15, the prophet writes "For thus says the High and Lofty one Who inhabits eternity, whose name is Holy: ...". So we know that eternity exists. One of Webster's Dictionary definitions of ***Eternity*** is: ***the timeless state into which the soul is believed to pass at death.***

Is there a heaven and a hell where you might spend eternity? The bible certainly declares **YES** to both questions. In fact, based on the Strongest Exhaustive Concordance of the Bible, there are 582 references of the word "heaven" and only 54 references of the word "hell". It should be interesting to ponder the question, "why are there 10 times as many references to "heaven" as to "hell"?

Let me ask this question another way. "Is there a heaven and a hell where you might spend eternity"? Let's address this question from a practical point of view. Let's look at the odds. Most people know what odds are. In horse racing, 20 to 1 odds are considered a long shot. This means that the maker of the odds is saying that they give a certain horse 1 chance in 20 races to win. Conversely, 2 to 1 odds means a given horse is given 1 chance in 2 races to win. This is the closest thing to "a sure thing". If you throw dice, you can understand how you have 1 chance or outcome in 6, to roll a given number. What about the various state lotteries, where the odds of winning the big bucks are at least a couple of million to 1? Somewhere I heard the new America Dream was to win the lottery.

A few of you may say, "I don't believe there is a heaven or a hell". Keep in mind something. It doesn't matter what you think! Again, let's look at the odds. There are only 3 chances or outcomes of the question, whether there is a heaven or hell. One chance is **Yes**, one chance is **No**, and a third chance is **Neither** a heaven or hell. You have 3 to 1 odds as the odds makers call it. Those of you who have ever gambled and those of you who have never gambled should understand my point. ***With 3 to 1 odds, why run the risk of going to hell?*** Webster defines ***hell*** as: ***1) the place or state of punishment of the wicked after death; the abode of evil or condemned spirits. 2) any place or state of torment or misery. 3) the abode of the dead; Sheol or Hades.***

Jesus was known to give many parables when teaching. A parable is defined as short-story designed to illustrate or teach some truth, religious principle or lesson. In the gospel of Luke 16:19-31, Jesus tells a story or a truth. ***This is not a parable***. This is a statement of fact from our Lord and Savior. Jesus talks about 2 people who are going to spend eternity in two different places. Read bible verses. Notice in these scriptures, that *torment* is mentioned four times. Webster defines ***torment*** as: ***1) to afflict with great, usually incessant or repeated bodily or mental suffering. 2) a state of great bodily or mental suffering; agony; misery.*** In verse 23 Read bible verse. In verse 24, Read bible verse. In verse 25, Read bible verse. In verses 27-28, Read bible verse.

So, for the last time, I'll ask the question, how long is eternity? Again, let's look at it from a practical point of view. A well know bible scholar and teacher gave an example of eternity's time measure that will be helpful in our thinking. Bear with me as I throw some rather large numbers at you, but they are necessary to make my point. The earth's sun is 93 million miles from earth, while the earth's moon is 240,000 miles from earth. The fastest measure of speed that man can actually calculate is the speed of light. Light speed is 186,000 miles per second, or 11,160,000 miles per hour. For light to travel from the earth to the surface of the moon, would take **1.29 seconds**. For light to travel from the earth to the sun, would take **8.33 minutes**. Now imagine all the grains of sand, on all the beaches of the earth. Can you picture that? Also imagine an eagle taking one grain of sand and flying to the sun. Now you know the eagle doesn't fly at 11,160,000 miles per hour. Can you picture that? Once the eagle deposits the grain of sand at the sun, he flies back to earth to get **another grain of sand**. The eagle does this until all the grains of sand, on all the beaches of the earth, have been deposit at the sun. ***This I submit to you is One day in eternity***. **Again I ask this question. With 3 to 1 odds that there is a hell, why take the risk?**

As I mentioned previously, Strong's Exhaustive Concordance has 582 occurrences of the word "heaven" and 54 occurrences of the word "hell". The word "heaven" is mentioned in 53 of the 66 books of the bible. Thirty-two books of the Old Testament and 21 books of the New Testament. From Genesis' "In the beginning, God created the heavens and the earth ...", to Malachi, where God is speaking, "If I will not open for you the windows of heaven and pour you out such blessing that there will not be room enough to receive it ...", to the seven parables in Matthew, where Jesus says "...the kingdom of heaven is like a man who sows good seed in his field", "... the kingdom of heaven is like a mustard seed ...", "...the kingdom of heaven is like leaven...", ...the kingdom if heaven is like a treasure hidden in a field...", "the kingdom of heaven is like merchant seeking a beautiful pearl...", "... the kingdom of heaven is like dragnet that was cast into the sea ..." to the Book of Revelation, "Now I saw a new heaven and new earth, for the first heaven and the first earth had passed away."

Of the 54 references of "hell", it is mentioned in 10 books of the Old Testament and 7 books of the New Testament. I'll use the one text in which Jesus said, "And this I say to you, that you are Peter, and on this rock I will build my church and the gates of hell (or Hades) shall not prevail against it."

As the bible clearly says, there is a heaven and a hell, and eternity awaits each and every one of us. In 2 Peter 3:8, it reads, 8 But, beloved, be not ignorant of this one thing, that one day *is* with the Lord as a thousand years, and a thousand years as one day.

The Power of Agreement in Marriage

I. *The Power of Agreement in Marriage*

Let's look at the title of this piece, "**The Power of Agreement in Marriage**", and examine the key words.

A. What does God's Word say about <u>power</u>?

Power – There are 272 references of "Power" in the Kings James Version of the bible. However, I believe one verse sums it up perfectly, which is found in Psalms 62:11, which says "...power belongeth unto God."

In **Matthew 16:19**, Jesus is speaking to Peter and he says, "And I will give unto thee the keys of the kingdom and of heaven: and whatsoever thou shalt bind on earth shall be bound in heaven: and whatsoever thou shalt loose on earth shall be loosed in heaven."

As Christians, and as married couples, we have the **POWER** to bind and to loose "whatsoever" in our marriage!

B. What does God's Word say about <u>agreement</u>?

Agreement – In Amos 3:3, God is speaking through the prophet Amos to the people of Israel, saying in verse 3, "Can two walk together, except they be agreed? In other words, God is saying, how can you walk with me, unless you agree with me?

In Matthew 18:19-20, Jesus says, "Again I say unto you, That if two of you shall agree on earth as touching any thing that they shall ask, it shall be done for them of my Father which is in heaven, 20: For where two or three are gathered together in my name, there am I in the midst of them."

In Genesis 11:5-6, it is written, "And the lord came down to see the city and the tower, which the children of men builded. 6: And the lord said, Behold, the people is one, and they have all one language; and they begin to do: and now nothing will be restrained from them, which they have imagined to do."

God, Jesus, and the Holy Spirit, had to come down from heaven to break up the agreement that the people had. For me and my wife, there is no other greater example of the power of agreement. Agreement is a spiritual law.

C. What does God's Word say about <u>marriage</u>?

Marriage – Genesis 2:20-24, it is written, "*20:* And Adam gave names to all cattle, and to the fowl of the air, and to every beast of the field; but for Adam there was not found an help meet for him.
21: And the LORD God caused a deep sleep to fall upon Adam and he slept: and he took one of his ribs, and closed up the flesh instead thereof;
22: And the rib, which the LORD God had taken from man, made he a woman, and brought her unto the man.
23: And Adam said, This is now bone of my bones, and flesh of my flesh: she shall be called Woman, because she was taken out of Man.
24: Therefore shall a man leave his father and his mother, and shall cleave unto his wife: and they shall be one flesh."

In Proverbs 12:4, it is written, "*4:* A virtuous woman is a crown to her husband: but she that maketh ashamed is as rottenness in his bones. In Proverbs 18:22, it is written, "*22:* Whoso findeth a wife findeth a good thing, and obtaineth favour of the LORD. In Proverbs 31:10, it is written, "*10:* Who can find a virtuous woman? for her price is far above rubies." In Ephesians 5:20-31, it is written, "*20:* Giving thanks always for all things unto God and the Father in the name of our Lord Jesus Christ;

21: Submitting yourselves one to another in the fear of God.

22: Wives, submit yourselves unto your own husbands, as unto the Lord.

23: For the husband is the head of the wife, even as Christ is the head of the church: and he is the saviour of the body.

24: Therefore as the church is subject unto Christ, so let the wives be to their own husbands in every thing.

25: Husbands, love your wives, even as Christ also loved the church, and gave himself for it;

26: That he might sanctify and cleanse it with the washing of water by the word,

27: That he might present it to himself a glorious church, not having spot, or wrinkle, or any such thing; but that it should be holy and without blemish.

28: So ought men to love their wives as their own bodies. He that loveth his wife loveth himself.

29: For no man ever yet hated his own flesh; but nourisheth and cherisheth it, even as the Lord the church:

30: For we are members of his body, of his flesh, and of his bones.

31: For this cause shall a man leave his father and mother, and shall be joined unto his wife, and they two shall be one flesh.

32: This is a great mystery: but I speak concerning Christ and the church.

33: Nevertheless let every one of you in particular so love his wife even as himself; and the wife see that she reverence her husband."

There is a prayer that we have for our unmarried son and two unmarried daughters, that he will find a wife and they will find a husband who loves God more then they love them, and that our son and two daughters will love God more they love their spouses. **This is the recipe for a God-blessed marriage.**

II. The Power and Agreement in Our Marriage

For Bertha and me, our largest segment of agreement in our marriage, is by far our prayer and worship time together each morning between 4-6AM. For the past few years at least, during a typical 30 day month, we may have missed praying together three or four times a month. When Bertha or I are praying, we say, "Yes Father", Yes Jesus, "Yes Holy Spirit", or "Thank You Father", "Thank You Jesus", "Thank You Holy Spirit", in agreement to what the other is praying. We usually read Proverbs for whatever day of the month it happens to be. I read it from the King James Version and Bertha reads it from the Amplified Bible, which adds richness to our reading of Proverbs. I challenge you to read Proverbs each and every day. Bertha and I know that you will experience a difference not only in your marriage, but in your daily aspects of life in relationship with God, yourself, and your fellow man. In our prayer and worship time, we agree that our children and our children's children will come to **know**, and **understand**, and **experience** God's Word **more perfectly**, so that they will be **doers of His Word** and not **hearers only.** We agree that other members of our family, friends, colleagues, even people we just met come to know, and understand, and experience God's Word more perfectly, so that they will be doers of His Word and not hearers only. My wife and I agree for good real estate listings, qualified buyers, our new home, and good real estate investments. We agree for marriages everyday, whether it is for a spouse for our unmarried children, couples that are currently married, but are experiencing difficulty in their marriages, or restoration of marriages. My wife and I **NOW** know that we have a marriage ministry.

III. Positive and Negative Powers of Agreement in Marriage

The Holy Spirit quickened my spirit a few years ago, letting me know that there are also negative powers of agreement. Think about it. If the husband or wife talks to another person about their marital situation in a negative way, and that person agrees with them, you have a negative power of agreement. The married person could be totally wrong about a given situation, or partially correct in knowing and understanding the facts of the situation, but now they are in agreement with that other person. Remember I mentioned to you earlier how so powerful the power of agreement was, that God had to come down and change that situation? Agreement with another person about your marital situation, or their marital situation, is still an agreement **for** or **against** your marriage or their marriage. **So, be very careful about what you say regarding another couple's marriage.** Your first response after you have listened to, and had spiritual discernment of the facts (please notice I said spiritual discernment. Ummmm, how do you get that?) should be, **"what does God's Word say about that situation?"** If you don't know what God's word says about the situation, **shut up**, and refer them to someone who does! **The result of an action or actions based on agreement in marriage or an agreement about a marriage will have the effect of dropping a pebble or a rock in a pond, lake, or ocean. There will be a rippling effect, be it positive or**

negative, for an unknown period of time! Let me give you an example of what I believe to be a positive effect in agreement in marriage. A few years ago, I decided that Bertha and I were going to the Gary Whetstone School of Biblical Studies. I was completing the application one evening and Bertha asked me what I was doing. I said, "We are going to bible school." She said OK. That was all she said. She didn't ask how, when, or how much it cost. She had spiritual discernment that let her know that going to bible school was OK (Ummmm, how do you get spiritual discernment?). Well, going to bible school blessed Bertha and me, but we didn't know that our action was instrumental in two other situations. We were at a subsequent **Marriage Advance**, which Victory Christian Fellowship has each year, sitting at the table with two newly wed couples. The couples were Terrance and Theresa, and Daniel and Denise. Theresa and Denise had been in bible school with Bertha and me for most of the two years, and both of them noticed our marriage. They both said to us that we were an example of what they wanted their marriage to be. Here is the point of our power of agreement. I strongly believe had Bertha and I not agreed to go to bible school, or expressed a negative attitude while attending bible school, we probably would not have been sitting at the table with them to hear the positive things they said about our marriage. I believe our power of agreement to attend and graduate from bible school not only produced a rippling effect that affected Theresa's and Denise's marriage, but blessed our marriage mightily in many other ways as well.

IV. If You Don't Like What You Are Receiving

If you don't like what you are **receiving** from your spouse, check on what you have been **giving** your spouse.

V. Your Marriage Is the Biggest Game Trophy Satan Can Get

There are only two institutions that God ordained – Marriage and the Church. Therefore, it stands to reason that Satan will bring all of his God-given power to bear against these two institutions. In Daniel 7:25, it is written *"25: And he (Satan) shall speak great words against the most High, and shall wear out the saints of the most High, and think to change times and laws: and they shall be given into his hand until a time and times and the dividing of time.*

However, in Ephesians 6:10-18, Paul writes *"10: Finally, my brethren, be strong in the Lord, and in the power of his might. 11: Put on the whole armor of God, that ye may be able to stand against the wiles of the devil.*

12: For we wrestle not against flesh and blood, but against principalities, against powers, against the rulers of the darkness of this world, against spiritual wickedness in high places. 13: Wherefore take unto you the whole armor of God, that ye may be able to withstand in the evil day, and having done all, to stand. 14: Stand therefore, having your loins girt about with truth, and having on the breastplate of righteousness; 15: And your feet shod with the preparation of the gospel of peace; 16: Above all, taking the shield of faith, wherewith ye shall be able to quench all the fiery darts of the wicked. 17: And take the helmet of salvation, and the sword of the Spirit, which is the word of God: 18: Praying always with all prayer and supplication in the Spirit, and watching thereunto with all perseverance and supplication for all saints;

Dr. Betty Price of Crenshaw Christian Center, where we

fellowshipped before coming to Victory Christian Fellowship, would say, be of one accord, one mind, one spirit, speaking the same thing, serving God, that we may come into the unity of the faith, and the fullness of the stature of Christ. She would say this addressing the congregation at Crenshaw Christian Center. *My wife and I say this to you, married couples, be of one accord, one mind, one spirit, speaking the same thing, serving God, that you may come into the unity of the faith, and the fullness of the stature of Christ.*

Don't allow Satan to hang your marriage on his trophy wall!!!

Be in **Agreement** for a God-blessed marriage. **God Bless You**!

Marriage Scriptures	Financial Scriptures	Faith Scriptures
I Corinthians 13	Malachi 3: 8-12	Hebrews 11: 1, 3, 6
Ephesians 5: 22-33	Luke 6: 38	Philippians 4: 13, 19
I Peter 3: 1-2, 7	2 Corinthians 9: 6-8	
Genesis 2: 21-24		
Deuteronomy 28: 1-14		

George R. Toulson, Sr.

November 2008

Traps of the Offended

Offense is defined as anger, resentment, hurt or displeasure. Spiritually, an offense on the born again believer can cause her/him to become entrapped by bitterness; Out of the place of security in Christ. Out of the "Secret Place of The Most High", as Psalms 91 describes, into the flesh where the enemy has control. Even though the Word tells us to "walk in the spirit" and not fulfill the lust of the flesh, when we are offended, the hurt, anger and resentment traps the believer and jeopardizes his standing with The Lord, His fellowman and himself/herself, as well.

As a wife, mother, sister, and church member, there have been many occasions to be offended. Women are considered "emotional"; Wives the weaker sex. According to the Word, husbands are alerted in this regard, 1 Peter 3:7, "Likewise You Husbands...". In other words, women are more susceptible to being offended. Once the offense has happened, if not dealt with according to God's Words, a root of bitterness which, if not bound and cast out, is the result. Eventually, "a stronghold" of the enemy can be constructed. Like a New York Ticker Tape, every time you think of the hurt, it is more difficult than the previous time to get rid of it. It goes around and around; you keep thinking about it over and over and over again. In particular, when you sit down to eat a meal, you will find that thought, that infraction, that hurt, coming back to you over and over again! It is little wonder why people eat too much or too little or eat or drink the wrong things. The Word tells us to stop the hurt or insult at the onset – the thought! (Phil 4:8). Heb 12:15 says, see that no root of bitterness spring up in you trouble you and thereby defile you.

In the world there was a popular recording, "It's a thin line between love and hate". There was even a movie made with that title. What was conveyed is between love mates. You can be in strong passionate love one minute, and then the next minute you are throwing hot grits, or burning up some one's clothing, or even in a place where one partner either kills another or is as passionately angry as he/she was in love. That kind of love is worldly, not at all Godly.

As a wife, you may have been ignored, or talked to sharply by your husband. What about after making passionate love the night before, you find yourself in a disagreement, and you feel like your husband was totally different from that night? You feel hurt and unappreciated, betrayed and maybe even misused. You feel as though he was not the same man as the one in your marriage bed. Your feelings are hurt. I remember George's former pastor saying, "Brother George, if "Bert" ever misbehaves as your wife, she is still your sister in Christ and must be treated as such". 1 Cor 13 tells you what love really is. Love is not a feeling – It is a commitment! Matt 22:40 says on the law of love hang all other commandments. Love your neighbor as yourself. When you exercise love, the love of God, there is no co-existence with hate. Love covers a multitude of faults and sins. In love, there is no competition or conflict. You relinquish your position (which in the natural you may be entitled to) for the other person. There are no harsh words. My girlfriend gave me good advice when she said, "Bertha, you can always say more later."

You don't try to crush another person with your words. JUST GOTTA GET IT OUT.

It was in the early 1980's when a young lady who obviously had seen my outward expressions to the events of some wrongdoing in a Church I had recently come to join, came up to me and said, "Bertha, offenses are a trap". That's all she said. She looked me straight in the eye on a Sunday and said again, "Bertha, offenses are a trap!"

Befuddled and disoriented as to how she knew my thoughts, I pondered my inward and outward appearances and concluded this as a "Word of Knowledge", "A Word of Wisdom" or "Discerning of Spirits". It was to my advantage, that the Lord would make me aware of some flaws in my own life which could cause my demise. For it was in that moment and probably many more, I <u>judged</u> this ministry. God is the Judge, and admonished me to keep my eyes on Him and not the vessels he had chosen for that ministry.

What happened to me, because of the Trap of Offenses, would take me on a long journey which would last twelve years, day in and day out trying to understand someone else's wrongdoing in my own eyesight. My entire life, ministry and career would careen in a downward spiral. In hurt and despair I prayed and cried, and wondered why God was allowing such abuse to happen in this church, not only to me, but to the hundreds and hundreds of other members, family and friends.

The Word of God tells us in Matt 7:1, "Judge not that ye be not judged". I knew that, but this is so obvious, Lord! Then I heard,

"Touch not my anointed (1 Ch 6:22) and do my prophets no harm". He said His gifts were without repentance. So long as the pastors stood before us, people were saved, delivered and set free. God had anointed them, just like He did Saul. I spent 12 years being injured day in and day out looking at all the maneuvers and strategies of the people. Leaving the church was not an option. I had to learn to survive my personal hurts, which drove me to God and the Holy Spirit. I found out I was there as an intercessor, which was my gift and anointing from God . So, I interceded. I had been trained in earlier years as a "gap warrior" based on Ezek 22:30, " I sought for a man among them, that should make up the hedge and stand in the gap before me for the Land'. So, I prayed without ceasing.

At that point, I knew why I had left a thriving ministry where everyone was flourishing and had come to this small, but vibrant ministry where everyone and everything was in my face. I could see the Pastors on their good days and their bad days. I could see how the church was growing by the multitude of salvations and deliverances. I could also see the "wounded soldiers". I needed to "Stand In The Gap"! I would dream of the pastors over and over again, and end up praying hours at a time. I told the pastors my dreams. And they would say, "Keep on praying Bertha".

There were Prayer Warriors in that church who thought it nothing to stay up all night praying in order to touch the heart of God and the life of the believer. We would come to the church at 5:00 in the morning even though sometime the pastors were not there to let us in. In the cold and dark, the

Prayer Warriors would stand outside and travail. Laying their hands on the fence. It was shocking to hear prophecies coming through the pastors which uncovered hidden sins and exposed Satan in an unprecedented way. Gang member turned in their head rags. Drug dealers brought their dope and guns in a display of true repentance. Prostitutes fell on the altar and became ushers and teachers.

The dichotomy, was now I see the fleshly side of God's chosen vessels. How was I going to handle that? Was I going to run to my old church 40 miles away from my new home. Was I going to seek another church close by? Was I going to murmur and complain and bring God's judgment on myself? What am I going to do? I decided to pray and watch God do what He does in me, the pastors, and the parishioners.

This morning, thinking on some current events here at Victory, I began to question some things. Actually, I was using my mind to make sense of them. – JUDGING! The Holy Spirit brought to my mind again, "Bertha, Offenses Are A Trap"! I thought about how only God knows the hearts and intents of man (1 Sam 16:7). I looked on the outside appearance. He reminded me of God's sovereignty. I heard in my spirit, how can you see the speck in your brother's eye, with that plank in yours

(Matt 7:3-5)?

As usually the oldest child at home out of a clan of 10, I was in charge of exacting out justice on my siblings based on listening to each side. I then reported to my parents in a detailed manner. They took care of the punishments based on my copious notes. When my parents chose a different conclusion than I surmised, I would voice my opinion (in a manner provided for only on Saturday Nights, where we all got to talk). Outside of those meetings, I got slapped in the mouth. When my parents argued, I was the referee and used the Bible as my authority. They didn't like that. They got divorced anyway.

As a high school student and later college student, I always asked questions. When I came to be a student of the Bible, I did the same thing. As a leader in Christian circles, I related to Moses and what a rough time he had with the Children of Israel. Why didn't he get to go into the Promised Land? I thought about the brother of the Prodigal Son. He was faithful to his father, yet the prodigal got the attention when he finally showed up. I understood the humanity of Martha, Mary's sister. How she always did the work while her sister sat around and enjoyed Jesus. Why is it that David was the apple of God's eye, even though he did so much wrong? Job was doing well until God reminded Satan of how blessed Job was. Then he lost everything - Why? Peter was only trying to let Jesus know how much he loved Him, but Jesus said, "thou art an offense to me". Why did Jacob get away with Esau's blessing? Remember the parable of the ten talents? Why did He take from the one and give to the guy who already had 10?

I don't know about you, but I have thought about these things. What about the person at work who got a promotion, while I worked like a slave and got nothing, but eventually fired? A Trap! Why God? Where is the justice in this? Many times in life,

I was hurt and had resentment about things that seemed unfair. I went on a campaign to change them. Who eventually got hurt was me! I don't know why bad things happen to good people.

What I do know is that God is good, all the time. He is all the while working in me both to will and do of His good pleasure (Phil 2:13). I know that God says I know the plans I have for you (Jer. 29:11, to prosper you and give you hope and a future). Why didn't I think about all the times He brought me out of situations I had no business being involved with? Did I remember the time when I was in the wrong place and could have been raped, but I called out the Name of Jesus and the perpetrator freed me? What about when the court judge did not find me in contempt of court, though it really could have been proven the other way? The Lord provided me with a blessed marriage, even though it was my <u>third time!</u> His love toward me said, "You will not be an outcast. I know your heart". When I think about the goodness of the Lord towards me, my soul cries Hallelujah! Thank you God for loving me! He is so faithful to help me raise six children as a single parent. It was God who made provision for me to return to Pepperdine University on a full scholarship, graduate summa cum laude, after the age of 32, while raising my own three children and on welfare.

I didn't mention how He delivered my daughter from a stroke last year when the doctors said, "ten patients have come in this hospital like her and she is the only one going out"! I don't know. The more I think I can figure God out, the more I find out what I don't know about Him, especially when I try to judge some other individual's life. God is Good! His Mercies endure forever! G-R-A-C-E, <u>God's</u> <u>Riches</u> <u>At</u> <u>Christ's</u> <u>Expense</u>.

The outcome of the ministry in the aforementioned church came to disaster. After some years, the pastors divorced and married other people two more times. They had each been married before at the onset of their marriage to each other. The parishioners scattered. Many went back to drugs, the street life, and many died. This is why I was called to pray! The wife began to preach out of her bitterness as a traveling evangelist. Much of what she preached was so tainted; it did not resemble the truth at all. The husband, who had actually abdicated his ministerial responsibility to the popular, animated, vocal in-demand wife, became so quiet no one knew where he was. He would never utter a negative word about his wife. He had a crippling fear of her threats and would barely show up to court appearances (even though this writer went). He went into seclusion. He found a multitude of counselors and repented to everyone he saw. The wife succumbed to a gruesome death after an ugly bout with cancer. Now in his sixties, the pastor has married a younger missionary and fathers three more babies, in addition to his four adult children. He is invited to minister at churches, many of which grew out of his original ministerial calling. Needless to say, most everyone had an opinion and expressed it. Some believed he was wrong, and she was justified and vice versa. **He did not let the offenses trap him.** On the other hand, some of the members became members of The First Church of The Offended, and had to repent and seek God in order to move forward. It took me twelve years.

In the media, some visible Christian marriages have been the focus, lately. Angry pastor couples are divorcing each other, even in physical altercations. I don't pretend to know their specific issues. They are offended. The root of bitterness had to have been there. The thought came, the hurt followed, went unchecked by the Word. The resulting stronghold was not dealt with. They fell into the trap.

Offences are a trap of the enemy. When we get into hurt, our walk with The Lord is compromised. In offenses, we take our eyes off God. We are attentive to a situation or another person. We may even judge someone else, our job, our church leaders, our family members. When we are caught up in looking at the circumstances, who is praying? One of the enemy's most clever tricks is to get our attention diverted. Then he comes in and steals, kills, and destroys our precious spouses, children, other family, our ministry, our church, our community. God is omniscient and omnipresent. He sees all, knows all and is everywhere and at the same time. He has no hands but our hands, no mouths but our mouths. He wants us to stand in the gap and intercede about everything. "Oh what peace we often forfeit, oh what needless pains we bear. All because we do not carry everything to God in prayer". I do know when all is said and done, God is the Judge, and judges righteously. He is not slack concerning His promises. What He says, He does (2 Peter 3:9)! I know He is Faithful. I know, when we walk in the spirit, we do not fulfill the lust of the flesh. (Gal 5:16).

I had always tried to figure seemingly injustices out and

couldn't. But let me go on record as saying, I asked God's forgiveness for judging. I repented for being hurt. I know I have been called to intercede in prayer. Now I am determined to move into the area of blessing others, as God has certainly blessed me. And stay away from the Trap of Offenses.

Humbly written by a work in progress,

Bertha Toulson.

October 2007

WHAT ARE YOU THINKING ABOUT

Thoughts

"Thoughts" are defined by Webster's Dictionary as the product of mental activity, consideration, attention, judgment, opinion, regard. We can have good thoughts or bad thoughts – Thoughts that foster life or brings death. We are to decide. **Proverbs 23:7** says as a man thinks in his heart, so is he. We are also told in **Deut 30:19**, "I call heaven and earth to record this day against you, that I have set before you life and death, blessing and cursing: therefore choose life, that both thou and thy seed may live". Choosing life, we need to ask ourselves moment by moment - **WHAT ARE YOU THINKING ABOUT?**

Controlling our thought life is done with offensive and defensive strategies: Pulling down strongholds, casting down imaginations; then renewing our minds. If this sounds like fighting, that's because it is. Thoughts come to us all the time. If we allow them, the same ugly thoughts will come time after time, like a New York Ticker Tape circling around and around with information on the stock market . Thoughts will come over and over and over again until we become so familiar with them that they form strongholds in our minds. (*Webster defines "stronghold" as 1. well-fortified place; 2. a place that serves as the center of a faction or of any group sharing certain opinion and attitudes*). With the passing of certain events, the thoughts you entertain will be vocalized or acted out. Strongholds – For example, someone offends you when they do or say something. The thought comes to your mind of what you would like to do the next time this happens; You didn't act on it, you just thought it. Unless you cast that thought down and replace it with the Word, you will say what you planned in your mind to say the next time the circumstances present themselves. You see we must take corrective action over our thoughts, if not, we will embarrass ourselves, hurt someone else and thereby disqualify ourselves as Christian witnesses. I ask you, **WHAT ARE YOU THINKING ABOUT?**

The thought comes to you, "Do I have cancer"? Where did that come from? Satan? Possibly. Certainly not God! Get into your fighting posture. Cast down the thought immediately (*Webster defines **"cast"** as 1. to throw or hurl; 3. to cause to fall; 6. to shed or drop*), then come back with the replacement action. The Word of God in **Isa 53:5** says, "But he was wounded for my transgressions, he was bruised for my iniquities: the chastisement of my peace was upon him: and with his stripes I am healed". What about, "are my children going to hell"? Grab that thought like you are wrestling a burglar, bind it and cast it down. Here comes corrective action. **Psalm 138:8** says, "The Lord will perfect that which concerneth me: thy mercy, O Lord, endureth forever: forsake not the works of thine own hands". **James 5:16** says, "...The effectual fervent prayer of a righteous man availeth much". **II Tim 1:7** says, "For God has not given me the spirit of fear; but of power, of love, and of a sound mind".

Have you ever wondered what would cause a person to commit the crime of murder? We gasp when hearing the news that a husband killed his wife; A mother drowned her children; The act of murder started with a thought. The thought was planted long before the action ever took place. When we think hateful thoughts, the scripture says we have committed murder already in our hearts. When discussing the subject of adultery, the bible says in **Matthew 5:27-28,** "Ye have heard that it was said by them of old time, Thou shalt not commit adultery: Vs 28: But I say unto you that whosoever looketh on a woman to lust after her hath committed adultery with her already in his heart". There is no such thing as it was an accident. It had happened in his heart, which came by way of his thought life.

I have stood by the refrigerator and tried to eat something though I was not hungry. Why was I standing there then if I weren't hungry? Satan? Maybe, but I am the one who has to take responsibility. Have you looked at a commercial on TV and all of a sudden you got hungry? Many times you wanted the exact thing you saw on the commercial. Advertising? Yes, but I am in control.

We never "arrive". Some pastors have thought they arrived only to find themselves in trouble with the law or in adultery which caused the church family to suffer in addition to their own family.

What Influences Our Thoughts

It depends if you are walking in the flesh or in the spirit. **Galatians 5:16-26** says, "... Walk in the Spirit, and ye shall not fulfill the lust of the flesh. Vs 17: For the flesh lusteth against the Spirit, and the Spirit against the flesh: and these are contrary the one to the other: so that ye cannot do the things that ye would. Vs 18: But if ye be led by the Spirit, ye are not under the law. Vs 19: Now the works of the flesh are manifest, which are these; Adultery, fornication, uncleanness, lasciviousness, Vs 20: Idolatry, witchcraft, hatred, variance, emulations, wrath, strife, seditions, heresies, Vs 21: Envyings, murders, drunkenness, revellings and such like: of the which I tell you before, as I have also told you in time past, that they which do such things shall not inherit the kingdom of God. Vs 22: But the fruit of the Spirit is love, joy, peace, longsuffering, gentleness, goodness, faith, Vs 23: Meekness, temperance: against such there is no law. Vs 24: And they that are Christ's have crucified the flesh with the affections and lusts. Vs 25: If we live in the Spirit, let us also walk in the Spirit. Vs 26: Let us not be desirous of vain glory, provoking one another and envying one another. **So, WHAT ARE YOU THINKING ABOUT?**

How Do we Control Our Thoughts

Thoughts can come from a variety of sources: In our study on the four sources of wisdom, we learned that thoughts come from God, satan, our own senses, and from the world.

Like a computer, we have to program our minds with the right information, so that we are not left with the negative consequences in life of acting inappropriately, living beneath our blessed inheritance or something worse.

How do we program the right information to our minds? The Bible tells us to renew our minds; **Romans 12:1-3** says "I beseech you therefore brethren, by the mercies of God, that ye present your bodies a living sacrifice, holy, acceptable unto God, which is your reasonable service. Vs 2: And be not conformed to this world: but be ye transformed by the renewing of your mind, that ye may prove what is that good, and acceptable, and perfect, will of God. Vs 3: For I say, through the grace given unto me, to every man that is among you, not to think of himself more highly than he ought to think; but to think soberly, according as God hath dealt to every man the measure of faith". Renewing the mind is a process which is attentive to each detail of every thought. Thoughts have to pass an acid test before they should be allowed to lodge in our minds. **Philippians 4:8** says "Finally, brethren, whatsoever things are true, whatsoever things are honest, whatsoever things are just, whatsoever things are pure, whatsoever things are lovely, whatsoever things are of good report; if there be any virtue, and if there be any praise, think on these things". Something may be true, but if it does not meet the other requirements of this scripture, like if there is no virtue or praise in it, the thought is not allowed. So I ask you, **WHAT ARE YOU THINKING ABOUT?**

Thoughts come to us like missiles all day long. We should have the "whole armor of God on" including our helmet of salvation, which would deflect the thought. But if the thought comes anyway, we have the Word of God to quench every fiery dart of the wicked one. **Joshua 1:8** says, "This book of the law shall not depart out of thy mouth; but thou shalt meditate therein day and night, that thou mayest observe to do according to all that is written therein: for then thou shalt make thy way prosperous and then thou shalt have good success".

My husband George and I wake up early in the morning to spend time in prayer and the reading of God's Word. This daily exercise builds us up in our spirit man and our soul. We are told in **III John 1:2,** "Beloved, I wish above all things that thou mayest prosper and be in health, even as thy soul prospereth". God wants us to prosper in all areas of our lives. He wants us happy.   God's Word changes our thoughts and conforms them to His thoughts. We then glorify God and bless our fellow man.

God cares about everything that concerns us. He desires to fellowship with us. In **Psalm 35:27 – 28** it says "Let them shout for joy and be glad, that favor my righteous cause: yea, let them say continually, Let the Lord be magnified, which has pleasure in the prosperity of his servant. Vs 28: And my tongue shall speak of thy righteousness and of thy praise all the day long".

Conclusion

Mankind was created to enjoy fellowship with God. We worship God in spirit and in truth. God's Word is His truth. The unrenewed mind is governed by the flesh. Flesh is diametrically opposed to the spirit. Our joy, happiness and prosperity are dependent on our walking in the spirit and continually taking authority over our thoughts. "For though we walk in the flesh, we do not war after the flesh". Renewing our minds is a constant process. George and I worship and praise God early in the morning, reading the scriptures which reinforce our Christian walk. We can laugh and enjoy fellowship with God and other people. George and I are not anxious or intimidated. We think no evil, therefore we speak no evil. We have joy, we have love, and that love affects and infects people around us. **So, WHAT ARE YOU THINKING ABOUT?** We are thinking about God! And behaving like Him. After all, He is Our Father.

ABOUT THE AUTHOR

You essentially know about the authors, as they are the subjects of this book. They are leaders at Victory Christian Fellowship Church in the Marriage Fellowship ministry and they rarely miss attending church each Sunday. Hopefully, their passion for marriage, their strong Christian faith, the prayers and spiritual pieces that the Holy Spirit has lead them to write, in addition to this book, and how God has blessed them exceedingly abundantly, give you a glimpse of their strong desire to be a blessing to the Body of Christ.

Made in the USA
Monee, IL
07 July 2026

56551670R00174